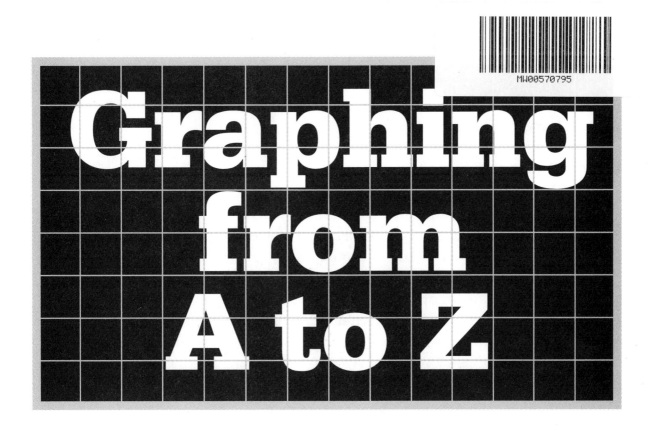

Graphing from A to Z

Written and photographed by Laurie DeVault, M.Ed.

Fearon Teacher Aids

A Division of Frank Schaffer Publications, Inc.

Dedication

For my son David, my greatest teacher

Acknowledgments

Many thanks to all who supported me during the writing and completion of this book, including the teachers and children who let me visit their classrooms. A special thanks to Ann Shea's first grade at the Fort River Elementary School in Amherst, and to Donna Covey and Paulette Levchuk's kindergarten at the Deerfield Elementary School in Deerfield. Thanks also to Laurie Hickson and Alan Arnoboldi, teachers of the Fort River Elementary School, for allowing me to photograph their children's graphs. And my deepest appreciation to Eddy Goldberg for moral and technical support, and to Linda Dodge, Louise Law, Amy Wolpin, and Margie Riddle for their excellent critiques and contributions.

Finally, love and thanks to all at the Whately Elementary school—especially Irene Branson, librarian extraordinaire, and to my wonderful kindergarten data collectors and their parents. And last, but never least, thanks to my dedicated and most patient teammate and frequent model, Maureen Antaya.

Editors: Kristin Eclov, Joanne Corker, Hanna Otero
Cover Design: Riley Wilkinson
Cover Photo: Riley Wilkinson
Illustration: Kelly McMahon
Book Design: Terry McGrath

© **Fearon Teacher Aids**
A Division of Frank Schaffer Publications, Inc.
23740 Hawthorne Boulevard
Torrance, CA 90505-5927

Fearon Teacher Aids products were formerly manufactured and distributed by American Teaching Aids, Inc., a subsidiary of Silver Burdett Ginn, and are now manufactured and distributed by Frank Schaffer Publications, Inc. FEARON, FEARON TEACHER AIDS, and the FEARON balloon logo are marks used under license from Simon & Schuster, Inc.

FE111030

Table of Contents

■ What Is Graphing?

From kindergartners sorting shoes to sixth graders making temperature charts on computers, graphing is rapidly gaining popularity in classrooms everywhere. Graphing is a dynamic process that begins with a question or hypothesis and involves data collection and analysis. When children graph, they organize information in exciting forms such as bar graphs, pie charts, and Venn diagrams. They learn to clarify, analyze, interpret, and apply all sorts of ordinary and extraordinary data!

Whether you are a veteran facilitator looking for more ways to use graphs in your curriculum or a first-year teacher unsure of where to begin, *Graphing from A to Z* will provide a useful tool for teaching graphing. Look through all of the original and creative ideas from A to Z before deciding which ones to try first. Some activities may be more appropriate for kindergartners, while others are better suited to second graders. Whatever your students' age group, you can adapt these ideas to meet their interests, needs, and abilities.

■ Collecting and Recording Data

With their natural curiosity about others, children enjoy the whole data collection process, whether at home, school, or in their communities. Beginning graphers need to experience a variety of ways to gather and record data so that they can learn what works best for different situations. They can observe, survey, count, or measure, and express their data as numbers (e.g., 74 pounds) or categories (e.g., purple). They can place their information on questionnaires, survey sheets, prepared graphs, and class lists.

They can record their data with:

• manipulatives (e.g., interlocking cubes, candy, pasta, counters, buttons, apples)
• attachments (e.g., sticky notes, name labels, child portraits)
• symbols (e.g., tally marks, check marks, lines, dots, X's, letters, numbers, names)

As your students work, encourage them to share and discuss their plans for collecting and recording their facts—and for dealing with additional or unexpected data.

■ Organizing and Presenting Data

Young children should experience and discuss a variety of graphic forms in order to learn how to organize and present data. They should begin with *real* or *object* graphs, and progress to *picture* (e.g., models) and *symbol* forms (e.g., X's, squares, numbers, words). Help your students use the same information in these different graphs so that they learn to make the connection between *concrete* and *symbolic*.

Whether your students use object, picture, or symbol graphs, they can present their data in various interesting formats.

• Bar graphs display data horizontally (in rows) or vertically (in columns) and help young children make simple comparisons between categories or quantities.

• Circle graphs (pie charts or graphs) show *parts of a whole* as each *slice* represents a portion of the whole *pie*. Circle graphs are difficult for young children to make on their own.

• Line graphs show changes that take place over time, such as the growth of a bean plant or daily temperatures. Line graphs can also be difficult for young children to understand or complete on their own.

• Venn diagrams use overlapping circles to present data that belongs in separate and shared categories.

■ Analyzing and Applying Data

Children find graphing much more meaningful when they talk about their data and use it in subsequent situations. For example, if your students are planning an ice cream picnic, they can survey, graph, and purchase their favorite flavors. Or, if all of the classes are raising funds to buy supplies for a homeless shelter, they can chart their progress with a giant bar graph at the school entrance.

When discussing a completed graph, include questions such as the following:

• What does the data show? What do you notice?
• Why do you think you got this data?
• Tell (or write) a sentence or story about this data.
• Which column or row has the most? Fewest?
• How many more (or fewer) are in the ___ column than in the ___ column?
• What if you did the survey tomorrow (next month, next season)? What about in another classroom, grade, or place? What would you find?
• What predictions can you make from this data?
• What conclusions can you make?
• What other questions do you want to ask?

© Fearon Teacher Aids FE111030

■ Assessment and Graphing

As the children work, you will find many ways to assess their learning. If they are new to graphing, begin slowly and guide them through each phase of the process. Early graphing experiences should be mostly hands-on, with a variety of opportunities to sort and classify objects and people. Older children can work at a more symbolic level and take more responsibility for collecting and organizing their own data.

■ Observations

Select a few students at a time to observe through the course of an activity. Use these suggestions to guide your observations.

Graphing Skills

• How are the students sorting and classifying? Do they notice similarities and differences? Do they notice details? Can they consider more than one attribute at a time?

• Do they use standard forms or their own ways to represent and display their data?

Work Habits

• Are the students' graphs clear and well organized? Are they creative?

• Do students print labels and titles neatly and correctly?

• How do they feel about their work?

• Do they cooperate with others and share ideas?

• Do they participate in discussions?

Application

• Can the students interpret data and make conclusions?

• Are their explanations reasonable and logical? Do they use supporting evidence?

• Can they make quantitative (numbers) and qualitative (types) observations?

• Can they interpret the data on other children's graphs? On unfamiliar graphs?

• Can they develop new hypotheses?

■ Documentation

As an essential part of your assessment, use some of these ideas to document the students' progress:

• Photocopy or photograph individual and group sorting and graphing worksheets and charts.

• Photograph or videotape the students as they collect and organize data.

• Have the students write or dictate their comments on the graphs.

• Encourage older students to document their reasoning in math journals throughout the process.

Graphing and the NCTM Standards

Most of the challenging requirements set forth in *Principles and Standards for School Mathematics*, published by the National Council of Teachers of Mathematics, can be addressed through graphing. For example:

- Children use a *problem-solving strategy* when they organize eye-color data into lists or use interlocking cubes to represent classmates on a bar graph.
- They *communicate* mathematical ideas when they discuss and display "favorite pizza" data on a circle graph.
- They develop *reasoning skills* when they analyze, organize, and interpret birth date data on a class graph.
- They make *connections* between mathematics and aspects of daily life when they graph money being raised for a class trip or survey peers about school uniforms.
- They develop *number sense* when they tally survey results about class pets or attach a numerical value to lines on a temperature graph.
- They make *estimates* when they predict and graph the number of buttons or zippers on their clothes.
- They deepen their understanding of *whole number operations* when they divide a bag of candy equally among themselves in order to graph the colors.
- They learn about *probability* and *statistics* when they toss dice or coins and graph the results.

"Quick" Graphs

Ideally, the students should actively participate in the entire data collection and analysis process. They should have frequent opportunities to decide what data to collect and how to collect it. They should also try different ways of representing and organizing the information.

Throughout this book, you will find many "quick" graphs, where students can place data (e.g., names, numbers, portraits, symbols) on previously prepared graph forms. Although these activities may take only a few moments to complete, they should be meaningful to students and discussed upon completion. Try to balance these quick ideas with unfamiliar graphing activities.

■ Graphing across the Curriculum

Graphing is not just for math time. Children can collect data almost anywhere, at any time, on any topic. Use this list of starting points to help you graph across the curriculum.

Language and Literature

- Graph the books students have read by number or type (for example, ask *How many "family" books have you read?*).

- Have students survey classmates and family members about literature (for example, have them ask *What was your favorite fairy tale story?*).

- Have students collect data on how classmates feel about characters, places, or plots (for example, have them ask *Which character in* Charlotte's Web *would you most like to be?*).

- Help students make Venn diagrams to compare different versions of the same tale (e.g., *Cinderella*).

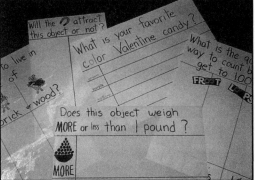

Social Studies

- Survey the class to assess prior knowledge about upcoming subjects (for example, ask *Do you know who Harriet Tubman was?*).

- Use personal surveys to help students get to know their classmates (for example, ask questions like *Who has a little brother?* or *Who eats oatmeal for breakfast?*).

- Have students collect data about family and community members (for example, have them ask questions like *What's your favorite TV show?* or *How old is your house?*).

Science

- Collect data to assess students' feelings and knowledge about upcoming topics (for example, ask *Do you like bats?*).

- Have students record and convey data from scientific investigations (for example, have them find out how far paper planes travel, how much baby hamsters weigh, or how tall tomato plants grow).

Health/Nutrition

- Have students collect data about health and nutrition (for example, how many times children brush their teeth daily or who has had chicken pox).

- Help students graph data from investigations (for example, how many grams of sugar are in breakfast cereals or how many calories are in favorite foods).

- Have students conduct safety surveys (for example, have them ask questions like *Do you wear seat belts?* or *Do you have smoke detectors at home?*).

Art

- Survey students about art categories such as color, form, shape, and texture (for example, ask *What shapes did you use on your mobiles?*).

- Have students share their opinions about their own art activities and other artists (for example, ask *Which book illustrator or painter do you like the best?*).

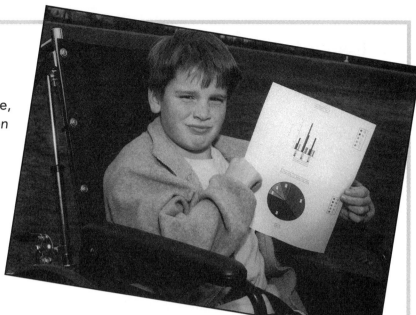

Music

- Use surveys to heighten students' awareness and generate interest (for example, ask *Do you know the folk song "Jenny Jenkins"?*).

- Have students find out about classmates' favorite songs, music, and instruments (for example, have them ask *What is your favorite song?*).

Physical Education

- Have the class graph their favorite P. E. and recess activities (for example, have them ask *What games do you like to play in summer?*).

- Help students collect data on game scores (for example, how many points a favorite team got during part of a season).

- Have each student graph his or her personal progress with assorted exercises (for example, how many sit-ups he or she can do in one minute).

Political/Social Action

- Have students conduct surveys and collect data to gauge opinions on certain school-wide issues (such as adding tacos on the school menu).

- Have students use graphs to chart their own progress and motivate others to help reach established goals (for example, how many books the class reads in a month).

- Have students find statistical information in newspapers and magazines to see how data is organized, displayed, and used to make decisions or influence people.

Technology

If you teach older students, have them use computer graphing programs after they have had experience making their own graphs.

■ Special Concerns and Issues

Since graphing involves personal data, use discretion when planning classroom activities. Be aware of sensitive issues related to family matters (e.g., parents, jobs, divorce, death, adoption, foster care, prison, illness), possessions (e.g., housing, toys, clothing), relationships (e.g., "best" friends), achievements (e.g., reading progress, sport scores), and physical data (e.g., height, weight).

Consider these suggestions:

- Use anonymous data if you feel that certain children may be embarrassed by information (e.g., weight, reading scores).

- Check the wording of questions or the designs of graphs for emotional bias. For example, avoid placing happy or sad faces in *Yes* or *No* columns in graphs about losing baby teeth or owning home computers.

- Be careful when asking questions related to celebrations and holidays such as Christmas, birthdays, and Thanksgiving.

■ Parental Involvement

Before you begin graphing, send home letters about the graphing activities and request the support of the students' family members. Parents and siblings may need to help count and record the number of beds in their homes, the ages of family members, or the length of their feet. You may choose to copy and use the sample letter on page 143.

Also involve parents in graphing activities during Open House and at parent conference time. Display student graphs around the room and invite parents to answer their children's questions and write down observations. When family members participate in data collecting, they learn more about what their children are doing and feel a stronger connection to the school.

■ Classroom Materials

Successful graphing can be enjoyed with simple ideas and everyday materials. Before you begin graphing activities, examine the following lists of resources.

Paper

Large pieces of chart paper or poster board
Long rolls of butcher paper or craft paper
Plain index cards (3½ inches x 5 inches, or 8.9 cm x 12.7 cm)
Copy paper (8½ inches x 11 inches, or 21.6 cm x 28 cm)
Sticky notes, assorted sizes and colors
Art paper

Manipulatives

Interlocking cubes
Blocks (pattern, shape, attribute)
Counters
Dice
Buttons, keys, shells
Plastic animals and toys

Uncooked beans and pasta
Stickers and sticky dots
Stamps (postage and rubber)
Plastic trays
Wooden clip-style clothespins

Miscellaneous Math Resources

Stopwatches or clocks
Balance and other scales
Graphing mats (store-bought or made from vinyl and masking tape)
Laminating film or clear self-adhesive plastic
Overhead projector, transparencies, and markers
Sorting or plastic hoops
Yarn or jump ropes
Tacks, picture hangers, or "sticky tack"
Magnetic strips or Velcro®
Small paper bags or plastic zipper bags
Pocket charts
Large storage boxes and folders
Calculators (older students)
Sorting and graphing computer software (older students)

Basic Art Supplies

These items will be referred to as *art supplies* and include markers, crayons, pencils, rulers, yardsticks, scissors, paper clips, clipboards, and tape (clear and masking).

■ A Few Final Tips

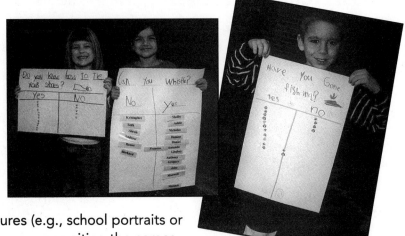

- Make and laminate some permanent generic or "Question of the Day" graphs (pages 88–89) to use throughout the year. These may include "Yes or No" graphs (pages 124–125) and "Would You Rather… ?" graphs (pages 88–89).

- Make reusable student portraits by placing small pictures (e.g., school portraits or ones you take yourself) on copy paper, writing the names underneath, and making numerous copies. Reduce sizes if necessary and cut and sort the portraits into class sets. You can also laminate the pictures or affix them to stiff paper.

- Prepare name cards by photocopying class lists on stiff paper. Laminate and cut the lists apart.

- Write the students' names on both sides of wooden clip-style clothespins so that they can be placed on the right or left side of two-column graphs.

- Place strips of Velcro® or magnetic tape in graph columns or rows and on the backs of data (e.g., children's name cards, portraits, numbers) for speedy graphing.

- Use an overhead projector to introduce sorting so that the children can watch the screen as you sort overhead transparency shapes and other materials.

- Make copies of the reproducible grids (pages 137–142) for the children to use with their graphing activities. You may use the grids vertically (in columns) or horizontally (in rows) to suit your activities, and add lines for names, titles, labels, and sentences.

- Encourage your children to sort data in different ways and create alternative graphs with the same data. As long as the data is clear, well organized, and labeled appropriately, unique graphs can be refreshing and thought-provoking!

- Model how to complete graphs with titles, labeled axes, and other pertinent information (e.g., keys, legends).

- Use tacks, picture hangers, paper clips, or "sticky tack" to display graphs on the wall.

Finally, keep in mind that completing graphs is only one part of an important and exciting process. If careful attention is paid to worthy mathematical goals, the graphing activities in your classroom will teach and inspire. So change, adapt, and extend all of these marvelous springboards to suit your students' needs. Let's go graphing!

It's Apple Season!

Materials

☑ Large chart paper or poster board

☑ Copies of Apples reproducible (page 128)

☑ Apples of various colors (one for each child)

☑ Sticky dots or masking tape

☑ Sentence strips or plain index cards

☑ Paper bag (optional)

☑ Art supplies

Apple activities are delicious—especially during harvest time! As manipulatives, apples and apple slices are versatile and easy to handle. In this activity, children organize apples to form colorful object and picture graphs.

Preparation

● Prepare a large four-column class graph on chart paper or poster board.

● Hand out copies of the Apples reproducible.

● Hide an apple in a bag and have students ask yes or no questions to guess what is inside the bag.

● Ask each child to bring an apple to school. Provide extras—especially rare yellow ones—to make sure that every child has an apple.

Collecting and Graphing

1. Give students time to examine their apples and sort them in different ways (e.g., size, color, stem/no stem).

2. Invite students to share observations (such as different apple colors); list their comments on the board.

3. Display the four-column graph and explain that the class is going to make an apple-color graph. Talk about how the apples could be grouped to show their different colors.

4. Help students print their names on sticky dots or strips of masking tape, affix them to their apples, and place their fruit in columns on the graph according to color.

5. Students can label the columns (e.g., Red, Yellow, Green, Mixed Colors) and title the graph What Color Is Your Apple?

6. Examine the object graph with the class and discuss the data. Write students' observations on sentence strips or index cards to display with the final graph. (For example, *My apple looks wrinkled. The mixed column has three more than the red column.*)

7. Provide the children with paper apples and ask them to color the paper apples to look like their real apples. They can write their names on their paper apples.

8. Have students take turns removing real apples and replacing them with paper ones. They should tape their paper apples in the appropriate columns on the graph.

9. Display the completed apple graph for students to examine and share.

Talking It Over

Discuss the two graphs (object and picture). Which one was easier to make? Which is easier to read? What is the same about both graphs? What is different? Did the data change when the real apples were replaced with the paper ones? What is the most common kind of apple? Least common? Why?

More Apple Fun

1. Display different colored apples and ask students which variety they think tastes the best. They can color paper apples to match their choices and place their data in the appropriate columns on a graph. Slice the apples into small pieces and invite the children to taste the different-colored fruit. Which is their favorite? They can color another set of paper apples to match their choices and place data in the appropriate columns on a second graph. Discuss the graphs. What is similar and different about them? How many children changed their minds after tasting the fruit?

2. Students can design and conduct a survey to answer the question, *How do you like your apple?* They can prepare a graph with three or four choices (e.g., *apple pie, apple sauce, apple cider, fresh apple*) and try to predict the outcome. The children can put their stickers, names, or portraits in their chosen columns. Have them discuss the completed graph and see how close their predictions were.

3. Students can cut fresh apples, dip them in paint, and make apple prints on paper. They can use these colorful shapes to record graph data.

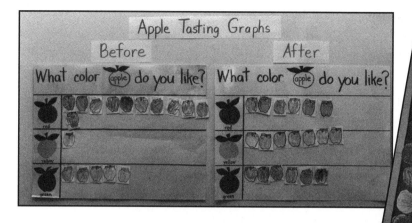

4. Challenge students to adapt popular tunes, rhymes, or games to the apple theme. For example:

(Tune: "Have You Ever Seen a Lassie?")
Have you ever seen an apple, an apple, an apple,
Have you ever seen an apple that grows on a tree?
A red one, a green one, a red one, a green one,
Have you ever seen an apple that grows on a tree?

The children can count and graph the number of apple words in their songs!

5. Read and discuss appealing stories such as the following:
   • *The Apple Pie Tree* by Zoe Hall (Scholastic, 1996)
   • *How Do Apples Grow?* by Betsy Maestro (HarperCollins, 1992)
   • *Johnny Appleseed* by Steven Kellog (Morrow, 1988)
   • *The Life and Times of the Apple* by Charles Micucci (Orchard Books, 1992)
   • *The Seasons of Arnold's Apple Tree* by Gail Gibbons (Harcourt Brace, 1984)
   • *Ten Apples up on Top!* by Theo LeSieg (Random House, 1961)

Students can graph their favorite apple stories and illustrations or find the books with the most apples. They can make apple-shaped graphs to report their information.

6. Invite students to be apple scientists and solve apple questions such as the following:
   • Will an apple float in water?
   • What happens when an apple is left on a plate by the window? (Provide options.)
   • What happens to a peeled apple? A buried apple? (Provide options.)
   • How much does an apple weigh? (Use standard or nonstandard options.)
   • Which fruit weighs more? (Provide an apple, an orange, and a banana.)

Students can graph predictions and results. They may use their portraits, name cards, apple stickers, or stamps to record their data.

Happy Birthday to You!

Materials

- ☑ Copies of Birthday Cake reproducible (page 129)
- ☑ Birthday items (e.g., cards, party hats, cakes, candles, gift wrap, gifts)
- ☑ Tray
- ☑ Assorted calendars
- ☑ Rope or clothesline
- ☑ Plain index cards
- ☑ Art supplies

Most children are interested in birthdays— especially their own! In this happy birthday activity, students place their birth dates on a class graph. If you have a child in class whose religious beliefs forbid birthday celebrations, use student portraits on the graph rather than birthday cake icons.

Preparation

- Hand out copies of the *Birthday Cake* reproducible.

- Place birthday items on a tray and ask students to guess why these objects go together. What is the grouping rule?

- Sing songs and chants related to birthdays and months, such as the following:
  Apples, peaches, pears, plums,
  Tell me when your birthday comes.
  January, February…

Collecting and Graphing

1. Display some calendars and talk about months and years. Ask students what happens on birthdays and why these days are important to people. When do students have their birthdays? How can they find out their birth dates?

2. Give each student a paper birthday cake to color and decorate. Each child can write his or her name on the top of the cake and his or her birth date in the middle. Students can also make their own "candles" to complete their decorations.

3. Tell students that they will make a special birth-date chart to display in the classroom all year long. Show the rope or clothesline and talk about ways to organize and attach the cakes. How should the students group their cakes? Should the cakes be in a certain sequence? Why? Should the chart start with September, like the school year, or with January, like the calendar year? Should the cakes in the same month be placed in a special order? Should the students include months without birthdays? Why or why not?

4. The children can work together to make column labels from index cards and title the graph *When Is Your Birthday?* or *When Were You Born?*

5. Display the hanging birthday graph for the children to share and examine.

Talking It Over

Discuss the graph. What does it show? Were there any surprises? Whose birthday is next? How many children have summer birthdays? Do any share a birthday? Whose birthday is in November? May? Were more students born in one month than in any others? Were more born in a particular season?

More Birthday Fun

1. If you work with an older class, have students work in groups to write plans for creating class birth-date graphs (e.g., taking turns to survey their classmates, using bar graphs with rows or columns, ordering data from January to December or from September to August). After collecting and recording their data, they can display their completed graphs. Group members can explain and discuss their findings with the class. Do they have the same data? What do they have in common? What is different? What works well in each graph? Students can write number sentences about their data to display with their graphs.

© Fearon Teacher Aids FE111030

2. Before lighting birthday candles, students can estimate how long (in minutes) the candles will burn. They can graph estimates and actual burning times. Be sure to discuss whose estimates were the closest!

3. Students can collect birthday data from other classrooms of the same grade level or from the entire school and then compare the information with their own class data.

4. Read books about months and birthdays such as the following:

   • *A Birthday for Frances* by Russell Hoban (HarperCollins, 1995)

   • *Chicken Soup with Rice* by Maurice Sendak (Scholastic, 1962)

   • *Happy Birthday, Moon* by Frank Asch (Simon & Schuster, 1982)

   • *Ice-Cold Birthday* by Maryann Cocca-Leffler (Grosset & Dunlap, 1992)

   • *Moira's Birthday* by Robert Munsch (Annick, 1987)

   • *Some Birthday!* by Patricia Polacco (Simon & Schuster, 1991)

   Students can graph their favorite birthday books, characters, illustrators, or covers. They can also answer specific questions related to the literature, such as *What gift would you buy the moon—a hat, a birthday cake, a rocket ship, or a pillow?*

Who's Got a Button?

Materials

- ☑ Shirt, sweater, or apron with many buttons
- ☑ Large chart paper or poster board
- ☑ Plain index cards
- ☑ Buttons (about 10 for each pair of students)
- ☑ Small plastic or paper bags (optional)
- ☑ Art supplies

Having a tub of buttons in your classroom is like having a treasure chest! Little fingers can spend hours admiring, feeling, counting, sorting, and making designs with these "jewels." Purchase bags of buttons from catalog companies and craft stores or solicit donations from parents, friends, and relatives. In this touch-and-feel activity, students work with partners to count how many buttons they're wearing and create a class graph with their data.

Preparation

For each pair of students, fill a plastic or paper bag with about ten buttons.

Collecting and Graphing

1. Wear an outfit with many buttons and challenge the children to estimate how many buttons you are wearing! Count the buttons to see whose estimate is the closest.

2. Talk about buttons and make a circular list of places where students might find them (e.g., on coats, cuffs, purses, pants).

3. Provide each pair of students with a bag of buttons and two index cards. Have the children write their names on the cards.

4. Challenge each student to guess how many buttons he or she is wearing without looking! Working together, partners can help count their buttons to see if their estimates were correct.

5. Students can count and glue the number of buttons they are wearing onto their cards. If they don't have buttons on their clothes, they can write zero on their cards.

19

6. Show students the chart paper or poster board and discuss how to collect, organize, and display the button data (index cards) on the paper.

7. Help the children group their cards appropriately (e.g., 0–5, 6–10) and glue them onto the class graph. They can help draw and label columns and add a button-decorated title such as *How Many Buttons Are You Wearing Today?*

8. Display the completed button graph for students to examine and share.

Talking It Over

Discuss the graph together. What do the students notice? How close were their estimates? What if they repeated this activity tomorrow, would they get the same data? What about on a cold winter's day? How many buttons would be on their coats?

More Button Fun

1. For a greater challenge, ask the children to estimate how many buttons are in the entire classroom. How can they find out for sure? Would a calculator help?

2. The children can sort and graph buttons according to different criteria (e.g., size, color, or number of holes). They can also use buttons in other math projects to model pattern making, addition, and subtraction.

3. Invite students to sit in a circle, and play the traditional game of "Button, Button, Who's Got the Button?" A volunteer moves around the circle, placing the button in a random student's hand and pretending to put it in the other students' hands while the class chants *Button, button, who's got the button?* Another child (designated to be "it") watches and makes five guesses to identify who actually has the button. If successful, that child takes a turn moving around the circle and pretending to hand out the button. Students can even graph the number of guesses their classmates make!

4. Read and enjoy books about buttons such as the following:

   • *The Button Box* by Margarette S. Reid (Penguin, 1990)

   • *Corduroy* by Don Freeman (Scholastic, 1968)

   • "The Lost Button" in *Frog and Toad Are Friends* by Arnold Lobel (HarperTrophy, 1970)

   • *Something from Nothing* by Phoebe Gilman (Scholastic, 1992)

   Students can graph their favorite button books or count and graph the total number of buttons in each book.

What's Your Favorite Color?

Materials

✔ Little color cards (e.g., teacher-made cards, paint chips, or linoleum samples)

✔ Books about color, such as the following:
  - *Colors of Mexico* by Lynn Ainsworth Olawsky (Carolrhoda, 1997)
  - *Kente Colors* by Debbi Chocolate (Walker Publishing, 1996)
  - *Let's Paint a Rainbow* by Eric Carle (Putnam, 1982)
  - *Purple, Green, and Yellow* by Robert Munsch (Annick, 1992)
  - *Who Said Red?* by Mary Serfozo (Margaret K. McElderry, 1988)

✔ Large chart paper or poster board

✔ Small, white paper rectangles

✔ Art supplies

Children love exploring the colors of the rainbow! In this activity, they create a class graph to show their favorite shades. You may use this idea when studying color and light in science or art.

Preparation

● Provide students with color cards. They can go on a "color hunt" outdoors and try to find colors that match their cards.

● Read and discuss colorful stories such as *Colors of Mexico* by Lynn Ainsworth Olawsky, *Kente Colors* by Debbi Chocolate, *Let's Paint a Rainbow* by Eric Carle, *Purple, Green, and Yellow* by Robert Munsch, and *Who Said Red?* by Mary Serfozo.

Collecting and Graphing

1. Talk about favorite colors. What colors do students like to wear? How do they like their bedrooms painted or decorated? What colors do they like on their bikes?

2. Provide students with small, white paper rectangles and talk about how they could use them to make a graph showing their favorite colors.

3. Have students use crayons to color their rectangles with their favorite colors (one color for each child) and write their names on their color cards.

 © Fearon Teacher Aids FE111030

4. Have students place their color data in the middle of the floor or on the board and examine it together. Is it easy or hard to tell how many children like certain colors? How can the class organize the cards to make it easier to count and compare them? Try some of these suggestions and discuss the results.

5. Help students place their color cards in rows or columns on the chart paper or poster board and make a graph. They can add lines, labels, and a title such as *What's Your Favorite Color?*

6. Display the completed color graph for students to examine and share.

Talking It Over

Discuss the graph together. What does it show? What is the shape of the data? What is the most popular color? Least popular? How many more children like one color than another?

More Color Fun

1. Challenge students to make number sentences about the color graph. They can write or dictate their ideas on sentence strips or index cards to display near the graph.

2. If you work with an older grade, have students do an all-school color graph and compare the findings with their own class graph. What are the similarities and differences?

3. Provide students with piles of small plastic toys (e.g., bears, cats, cars) in four different colors. They can use these toys to make object graphs of their favorite colors.

4. Have students survey their families about favorite colors. They can use their data to make individual graphs or pool their findings to make a large class graph. What do the graphs show? What is their shape? Is one color still the most popular? What are the most or least popular colors?

5. Challenge students to find color words in songs and books such as "Colors" by Hap Palmer (*Learning Basic Skills through Music, Volume 1*, Educational Activities, 1969) or the traditional "Jenny Jenkins" (*Folksingers Wordbook*, Oak Publications, 1973). They can graph their favorite color songs or books or see what color words appear most frequently.

Pick a Bear! what color did you pick

It's Time for a Cookie!

Materials

- ☑ Three types of cookies (e.g., chocolate chip, peanut butter, oatmeal. When choosing cookies, be aware of food allergies!)
- ☑ Paper bag (optional)
- ☑ Small paper plates or napkins
- ☑ Cookie-size pieces of paper
- ☑ Large chart paper or poster board
- ☑ Art supplies

Who doesn't love cookies? Perhaps the best way to reach children's minds is through their tummies—and eating and graphing cookies is a sure hit! In this yummy activity, children select their favorite cookies, and create a graph to show the top choices.

Preparation

- Hide a cookie in a paper bag and have students ask *yes* or *no* questions to discover the bag's contents.

- Arrange three types of cookies—in pieces or mini-cookie size—on paper plates.

Collecting and Graphing

1. Talk about cookies. How many kinds can the children list? Where do they get cookies? Have they ever made them? What sort would they like to eat right now?

2. Display the three types of cookies. The children can have a cookie taste test and choose their favorites.

3. Provide students with cookie-size paper and ask them to draw and color their favorite cookies (one for each child). They can print their names on their "cookies."

4. Show students the chart paper or poster board and talk about ways to organize the cookie data to make a graph.

5. Students can help draw three columns on the paper and glue or tape their cookies in the appropriate sections. They can also add column labels and a title such as *What's Your Favorite Cookie?*

6. Display the completed cookie graph for students to examine and share.

Talking It Over

Discuss the graph together. What does it show? Which was the favorite cookie? Which was least favorite? Why? How many more or fewer like one cookie than another? Did anyone predict the favorite cookie? What would happen if they surveyed another class? Who might be interested in this information? What about their families? Do all of their family members like the same cookies as they do?

More Cookie Fun

1. Perform this popular chanting game together:

   Class: Who stole the cookie from the cookie jar?
   First child: (Second child's name) stole the cookie from the cookie jar!
   Second child: Who me?
   Class: Yes, you!
   Second child: Couldn't be!
   Class: Then who?
   Second child: (Third child's name) stole the cookie from the cookie jar!
   Repeat several times.

2. Students can write number sentences about their cookie data. They may use numbers or terms such as *most popular, least popular,* and *equal amount.* (For example, *Twelve more people like chocolate chip than oatmeal cookies. Half the class likes ginger snaps.*)

3. Ask students to survey their family members, find their favorite cookies, and make graphs to share their data with classmates.

4. With adult assistance, the children can bake chocolate chip or other cookies in the classroom. They can sell their goodies to raise funds for something special (e.g., a field trip, a class pet) and graph the amount of money earned from the sale. They can even count and graph the number of chocolate chips in their cookies!

5. Students can read and dramatize popular cookie stories such as *If You Give a Mouse a Cookie* by Laura Joffe Numeroff (Scholastic, 1985) and *The Doorbell Rang* by Pat Hutchins (Mulberry, 1986). In the latter, they can figure out how many cookies each story character gets. They can also make their own finger puppets for the retellings.

Counter Toss Game

Tossing coins and dice is always fun because of the element of surprise. In this statistical activity, students learn about probability as they toss two-color counters ten times and graph the results.

Preparation

Hand out one copy of the *Two-Column/Row Grid* reproducible for each pair of students. Before copying, add a title and lines for students to write their names and sentences about the activity.

Collecting and Graphing

1. Display a simple two-color counter. Invite students to predict what color will show when you toss the counter down.

2. Throw the counter and discuss the results. Did your students really know which color would show? Why not? What if you toss it again? How about if you toss it ten times? Will one color show up more often than the other?

3. Provide each pair of students with a two-color counter and a grid page. Explain that they are going to take turns tossing their counters ten times.

4. Demonstrate how to record the color of each toss by placing X's in the appropriate columns on the grid.

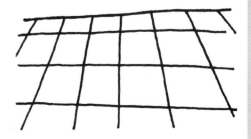

5. Before they begin, the children can predict how many of each color they will get from ten tosses. (This helps reinforce number combination facts for ten.)

6. After ten tosses, the children can stop and tally their results. They can also write or dictate one or two sentences about the data. (For example, *My prediction was right. We got more reds! We got seven reds and three yellows.*)

Talking It Over

Discuss the activity together. What did the children find? What do their graphs look like? Did they get more of one color than the other? Would they get the same results if they repeated the activity? Did different pairs of children get similar data? What might happen if they put all of the data together in a class graph?

More Counter Fun

1. Have the class sit in a circle and give each student a counter. Tell them that they are all going to make one toss. Can they predict the results? Will there be more of one color than the other? Have the children toss their counters in front of them. What happens? They can graph their results by placing their counters on a large graph in the middle of the circle. Repeat the activity and compare the results.

2. Use two-color counters to help reinforce number combinations and probability. For example, when working on the number 7, students should use seven counters to make their ten tosses. With each toss, they can write the resulting equation (e.g., *5 blue + 2 red = 7 counters, 7 yellow + 0 green = 7 counters*). Is there a higher frequency of certain combinations? Why might this be?

Do You Have a Dog?

Materials

☑ Large chart paper or poster board

☑ Books about dogs, such as the following:
  - *Arthur's New Puppy* by Marc Brown (Trumpet Club, 1993)
  - *Good Dog, Carl* by Alexander Day (Scholastic, 1985)
  - *I'll Always Love You* by Hans Wilhelm (Scholastic, 1985)

☑ Student name cards or portraits

☑ Art supplies

Most children love dogs or cats, and they usually enjoy talking about their four-legged friends! In this activity, students complete a class graph to show who does—and who doesn't—have a dog.

Preparation

Prepare a large two-column graph from the chart paper or poster board.

Collecting and Graphing

1. Share some popular dog stories such as *Arthur's New Puppy* by Marc Brown, *Good Dog, Carl* by Alexander Day, and *I'll Always Love You* by Hans Wilhelm. Ask how many students have dogs, and encourage them to talk about their pets.

2. Show the prepared two-column graph and provide students with name cards or portraits. Tell students that they will help create a graph to tell for sure how many class members do and do not have dogs.

3. Ask the class for their suggestions about how to complete the graph. Try out some of their ideas, and label the columns *Yes* and *No*. Give the graph a title such as *Do You Have a Dog?*

4. Students can take turns taping or gluing their photos or names in the appropriate columns.

5. Display the completed canine graph for students to examine and share.

Talking It Over

Discuss the graph. What does it show? Did it turn out as the students had expected? Can they tell how many dogs everyone has altogether? Some children may assume that each person in the *Yes* column has just one dog. Point out that the data doesn't show how many dogs each student owns; it simply shows the number of students that own dogs. Ask how the class could find out how many dogs each student owns.

More Dog and Cat Fun

1. Students can repeat the activity to make a class graph titled *Do You Have a Cat?* and compare dog and cat data. What is the same about the two graphs? What is different? They can also make a class Venn diagram to show who has a dog, a cat, or both.

2. Have students sort and graph little plastic dogs or cats (available through catalog companies) according to attributes such as color, size, and breed. They can also sort the plastic toys according to a mystery rule and see if classmates can guess the rule.

3. Students can use standard and nonstandard measures to collect physical data about their cats and dogs. They can measure lengths and heights, find weights, count colors, and chart ages to find "typical" dog or cat data.

4. Invite students to "survey" their pets to discover the most popular dog or cat food or treats and have them make graphs with the data. Who may be interested in these results?

5. Read and discuss dog or cat stories and songs such as the following:

   - *Dogzilla* by Dav Pilkey (Harcourt Brace, 1993)

   - *The First Dog* by Jan Brett (Harcourt Brace Jovanovich, 1988)

   - *Harry the Dirty Dog* by Gene Zion (HarperTrophy, 1976)

   - "I Wanna Be a Dog" by Charlotte Diamond (*Ten Carrot Diamond*, Charlotte Diamond Music, 1985)

   - *Naming the Cat* by Laurence Pringle (Walker, 1997)

   - *No More Fleas* by Anne Peutrell (Barron's Educational Services, 1999)

   - *Three Names* by Patricia MacLachlan (Zolotow, 1991)

   Students can graph their favorite dog or cat stories or characters, the saddest or funniest tales, and the best covers or animal illustrations.

What Color Are Your Eyes?

In this "eye-opener," students collect data to create a class eye-color graph. You may use this special activity with the eye-glass activity (pages 36–37) or when studying eye care and sight in science or health.

Materials

- ☑ Large chart paper or poster board
- ☑ Copies of Eyes reproducible (page 130)
- ☑ Blindfolds
- ☑ Books about seeing, such as the following:
  - I Am Eyes, Ni Macho by Leila Ward (Scholastic, 1978)
  - I Can Read with My Eyes Shut! by Dr. Seuss (Random House, 1978)
- ☑ Small hand mirrors
- ☑ Art paper or plain index cards
- ☑ Art supplies

Preparation

- For younger children, prepare a large graph from the chart paper or poster board by making columns for different eye colors in the class.

- Hand out copies of the Eyes reproducible.

- Have students pair up and take turns wearing blindfolds and going on "trust" walks around the classroom. They can try to identify objects, sounds, and friends without the aid of sight.

- Read a story about seeing such as I Am Eyes, Ni Macho by Leila Ward or I Can Read with My Eyes Shut! by Dr. Seuss.

Collecting and Graphing

1. Talk about eyes. What do children need to see? Like to see? Can everyone see? Do all eyes look the same? What makes them different? How should they care for their eyes?

2. Ask students to look into their friends' eyes. What do they notice? Pass out small hand mirrors and have students study their own eyes. What colors do they see? If necessary, help them identify colors such as gray, hazel, or green.

3. Invite students to guess how many different eye colors there are in their class. How can they find out exactly? Discuss some of these ideas.

4. If you are working with younger children, show the prepared graph with columns for different eye colors. Provide them with eye pictograms to color and place on the graph. They can also help label the columns and add a title.

5. Older children can draw their eyes on small index cards or art paper and work together to organize and display the data on the chart paper or poster board.

6. Display the completed eye-color graph for students to examine and share.

Talking It Over

Discuss the graph together. What does the data show? Is it what students expected? What is the most common color? What is the least common? Who has the same color eyes? Who has eyes that are different colors?

More Eye Fun

1. Hand out copies of the *Survey* reproducible (page 133) and have students "survey" their pets and/or toys to find their eye colors. They can make individual graphs about their eye-color data to share with the class.

2. Read books about eyes and the joy of sight, such as the following:

   • *Brown Bear, Brown Bear, What Do You See?* by Bill Martin, Jr. (Henry Holt, 1983)

   • *The Eye Book* by Theo LeSieg (Random House, 1968)

   • *I Went Walking* by Sue Williams (Gulliver, 1989)

   • *Knots on a Counting Rope* by Bill Martin Jr. and John Archambault (Trumpet Club, 1987)

   • *Look Closer!* by Peter Ziebel (Clarion, 1989)

   • *Naomi Knows It's Springtime* by Virginia Kroll (Boyds Mill, 1993)

   • *People* by Peter Spier (Delacorte, 1980)

   • *Two Eyes, A Nose, and a Mouth* by Roberta Grobel Intrater (Scholastic, 1995)

   • *We Are All Alike… We Are All Different* by the Cheltenham Elementary School Kindergartners (Scholastic, 1991)

Students can graph their favorite eye books, covers, or illustrators— or count, tally, and graph the number of eyes in their books! Once again, they may even include toys in their tally.

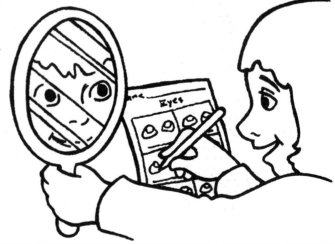

Family Fun!

Materials

☑ Overhead projector (optional)

☑ Overhead projector transparency (optional)

☑ Overhead projector markers (optional)

☑ Large pieces of chart paper or poster board

☑ Books about families, such as the following:
  • All Kinds of Families by Norma Simon (Albert Whitman, 1976)
  • Big Book of Families by Catherine and Laurence Anholt (Candlewick, 1998)
  • Brothers and Sisters by Ellen B. Senisi (Cartwheel, 1993)
  • Con Mi Hermano/With My Brother by Eileen Roe (Scholastic, 1991)
  • On Mother's Lap by Ann Herbert Scott (Scholastic, 1972)

☑ Sticky notes or plain index cards

☑ Class list

☑ Art supplies

Your students may be members of "traditional" families or may live with one parent, parents of the same gender, grandparents, guardians, or step-parents. Whatever the situation, they can collect all sorts of family data. In this sibling activity, students count the number of brothers and sisters in their families and make individual or whole-class graphs.

Preparation

● Make an overhead transparency of the class list or print it on a large chart. (Include your own name.)

● Read and discuss stories about families such as *All Kinds of Families* by Norma Simon, *Big Book of Families* by Catherine and Laurence Anholt, *Brothers and Sisters* by Ellen B. Senisi, *Con Mi Hermano/With My Brother* by Eileen Roe, and *On Mother's Lap* by Ann Herbert Scott.

Collecting and Graphing

1. Talk about what makes families special. Are all families the same? What makes them different? What about brothers and sisters? Does everyone have a sibling? Do students all have the same number of brothers and sisters? How could they make a class graph about their siblings?

2. Share ways to count brothers and sisters. Use your fingers to tally your own siblings; don't count yourself. (If you have no siblings, demonstrate the use of zero.)

3. Have each student count his or her siblings. They can draw or write their answers on sticky notes or index cards. How could they put all this data together to make a class graph?

4. Show the chart or overhead transparency and, at the top, write *How many brothers and sisters do you have?* Go through the class list and write the number of siblings next to each child's name.

5. Examine and discuss the completed chart. What do students notice? How could they group the numbers in columns to make it easier to compare them? How should they represent the data? (Ideas may include using names, sticky notes, dots, and X's.)

6. Students can help draw and label columns and count the numbers on the class list. They can place the data in the appropriate columns and add a title such as *How Many Brothers and Sisters Do You Have?*

7. Display the completed sibling graph for students to examine and share.

Talking It Over

Discuss the graph. Is the data easier to understand when it's grouped together this way? What is the largest number of siblings? Is there one number that comes up most often? What is the range of numbers? How many students have no siblings? Could this data change over time? Can the children tell how many brothers and sisters each student has? How could they find this out? Can they tell which siblings are brothers and which are sisters? How could they find out?

More Family Fun

1. Students can complete simple graphs or Venn diagrams to answer other family questions such as the following:

    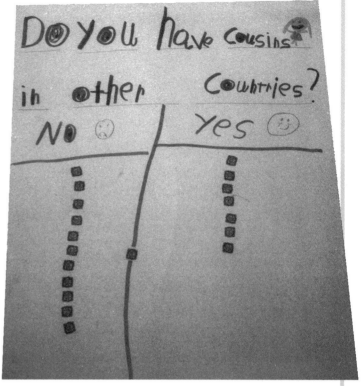

    - How many people are in your family?

    - Do you have a brother and/or sister?

    - How many brothers and/or sisters do you have?

    - How many cousins do you have?

    - How many aunts and/or uncles do you have?

    - Do you have cousins in other countries?

2. If you work with older students, have them collect data about the characteristics of family members (e.g., height, age, hair color, birthdays, birth places). They can also interview family members about their preferences or opinions (e.g., favorite foods, movies, colors, books). Students can share their data with classmates and pool information to make whole-class family graphs.

3. Invite students to collect data about the holidays they celebrate and their ancestral roots. They can transfer their data onto festive class graphs. (Be aware of children who do not celebrate certain holidays and of those who are adopted or in foster care.)

4. Enjoy reading many other family books such as the following:

    - *Families* by Meredith Tax (Joy Street, 1981)

    - *I Love My Family* by Wade Hudson (Scholastic, 1993)

    - *Loving* by Ann Morris (Lothrop, Lee & Shepard, 1990)

    - *Noisy Nora* by Rosemary Wells (Dial, 1973)

    Students can graph their favorite family books, covers, illustrations, or characters. They can also respond to specific questions about the story or choose the storybook family they'd like to visit.

How Many Feet?

Materials

- ☑ Interlocking cubes
- ☑ Glue bottles (about 10)
- ☑ Paper towel rolls (about 10)
- ☑ Large chart paper or poster board
- ☑ How Big Is a Foot? by Ralph Myller (Bantam, Doubleday, Dell, 1990)
- ☑ Three paper crowns (optional)
- ☑ 12-inch shoe
- ☑ Long length of chart paper or poster board
- ☑ Art supplies

After students have used nonstandard measuring materials (e.g., interlocking cubes, rods, coffee scoops, soup cans), they can begin learning about standard units such as feet, inches, and meters. In this activity, children use interlocking cubes to measure their feet and organize their results on a class graph.

Preparation

Challenge students to measure the length of a table (or your height!), first using interlocking cubes, then glue bottles, and, finally, paper towel rolls. They can graph the data and discuss why it takes more cubes than tubes to equal the length of the item being measured.

Collecting and Graphing

1. Provide three volunteers with crowns and dramatize How Big Is a Foot? by Ralph Myller. This is the hilarious story of what happens when a king does not use standardized measurements to make a bed for his wife! Use a foot-long shoe to help the children see how feet can differ in length and measurement (inches and centimeters).

2. Place the length of paper on the floor and model how to measure your foot with cubes. Explain that students are going to use interlocking cubes to measure their own feet. Decide whether to leave shoes on or take them off.

3. Have students work in pairs to measure their feet with the cubes. They can assemble their "cube feet" and bring them to the paper on the floor.

4. Help students organize their "cube feet" into columns, placing them in order from shortest to longest on the paper.

5. Explain that the class has just made an object graph!

Talking It Over

Discuss the graph. What do the students notice? What is the shape of the data? What is the range? Is there a foot length that most children in the class seem to have? Would they find similar data in another classroom? What may happen if they repeated the graph at the end of the year? Next year?

More Foot Fun

1. Students can trace around their feet and place the paper feet in order from smallest to largest. What does their graph show? What's the range of the data? Who has the smallest foot? The largest?

2. Ask students to measure the feet of their family members. They can graph and share their results with the class. They can also count all of the feet in their home, including those of pets. Discuss how to graph this data. Adventurous children may even count the feet of their toys!

3. Have students sort and graph assorted classroom items that are less than, the same as, and greater than one foot, or 30 centimeters, in length. They can also use other standardized measures, or their own feet.

4. Find and share books about feet and toes such as the following:

   • *Busy Toes* by C. W. Bowie (Charlesbridge, 1998)

   • *Can You Count Ten Toes?: Count to 10 in 10 Different Languages* by Lezlie Evans (Houghton Mifflin, 1999)

   • *The Foot Book* by Dr. Seuss (Random House, 1968)

   • *Hello Toes! Hello Feet!* by Ann Whitford Paul (D. K. Publishing, 1998)

   • *My Feet* by Aliki (HarperCollins, 1992)

   The children can graph their funniest foot or toe books—or count and graph the number of feet in the books.

Do You Wear Glasses?

Materials

☑ Large chart paper or poster board or a "Yes or No" graph (pages 124–125)

☑ Copies of Survey reproducible (page 133)

☑ Assorted eyewear (e.g., reading glasses, safety glasses, contact lenses, sunglasses)

☑ Student name cards or portraits

☑ Art supplies

In this "spectacular" activity, students conduct surveys to see who wears—and who doesn't wear—eyeglasses. They can collect their data in the classroom as well as at home. Do this special activity at the same time as the eye-color graph activity (pages 29–30) or when a student gets his or her first pair of glasses.

Preparation

● Prepare a large two-column graph from the chart paper or poster board.

● Hand out copies of the Survey reproducible. If you work with younger children, print a question (e.g., Do you wear glasses?) and column labels (Yes, No) on the page before copying.

Collecting and Graphing

1. Display assorted eyewear and discuss why people need to wear each type. If you wear glasses or contact lenses, describe how they help you. Also invite students to talk about family members who wear glasses and why they wear them. Encourage glasses-wearers in the class to share their stories.

2. Tell students that they will create different graphs—a class graph and family graphs—to show who wears glasses and who doesn't.

3. For the class graph, display the large two-column graph and give students their name cards or portraits. Invite them to place their names or pictures in the appropriate columns.

4. Students can label the columns (Yes, No) unless you use a generic "Yes or No" graph. They can also help title the graph Do You Wear Glasses?

5. For the individual family graphs, provide students with surveys and show them how to write the names of their family members in the Yes or No columns. (They may complete this activity for homework.)

6. Display the completed class and family eyeglasses graphs for students to examine and share.

Talking It Over

Ask students what they notice about the class graph. How many students wear or don't wear glasses? Do they think the graph will change in five years? In ten years? Why? Discuss what kinds of data change (e.g., height, shoe size) and what kinds remain the same (e.g., eye color, gender).

Have students analyze their family data. How many members wear or don't wear glasses? Did students remember to include themselves in the family graphs? Are there more people who wear glasses than who don't in their families? Do they notice any patterns? Do more parents or more children wear glasses? Do parents who wear glasses have children who wear glasses? How could the children group all of the family data together into one graph? Explore the possibilities and try some of the ideas.

More Glasses Fun

1. Take a look at books about wearing glasses, such as the following:

   • *Arthur's Eyes* by Marc Brown (Little, Brown, 1979)

   • *All the Better to See You With!* by Margaret Wild (Albert Whitman, 1993)

   • *Glasses for D. W.* by Marc Brown (Random House, 1996)

   • *Katie's Magic Glasses* by Jane Goodsell (Houghton Mifflin, 1965)

   • *Spectacles* by Ellen Raskin (Macmillan, 1968)

   Students can graph their favorite books, covers, characters, or spectacles. They can also respond to specific questions about the stories.

2. Discuss what might happen if students surveyed all of the classes and made an all-school graph. Help them perform this survey, then display the graph. What do they notice about the data? Does it change as children get older? How?

3. Just for fun, display three decorative pairs of glasses and ask students to select and graph the silliest, prettiest, or most colorful pairs.

4. Talk about visual impairments and handicaps. Invite a visually impaired person to visit and discuss how he or she lives. Students can also graph responses to specific questions about eye care and safety (e.g., how to handle sharp objects, protecting eyes from the sun).

What's in Your Grab Bag?

Materials

- ✔ Small plastic zipper bags, one for each child

- ✔ Small objects (e.g., beads, keys, pasta, buttons, used postage stamps, bottle caps, lids, toy animals, beans, seeds)

- ✔ Copies of Three-Column/Row Grid reproducible (page 138)

- ✔ Large piece of chart paper or poster board (optional)

- ✔ Larger objects such as pattern blocks, crayons, markers, large sea shells, large blocks, or toy animals (optional)

- ✔ Plastic trays or sorting hoops

- ✔ Art supplies

Curious children love exploring the contents of grab bags! They can work independently to graph the objects in different categories such as size, shape, color, or texture.

Preparation

- ● Fill each plastic bag with 9–12 small objects.

- ● Hand out copies of the *Three-Column/ Row Grid* reproducible. If you work with younger children, add your own title, labels, lines, and instructions before copying.

- ● Prepare an enlarged copy of the reproducible grid on the chart paper or poster board.

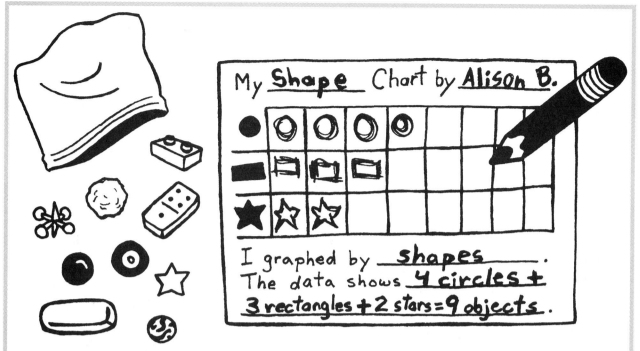

My **Shape** Chart by **Alison B.**

I graphed by **shapes**.
The data shows **4 circles + 3 rectangles + 2 stars = 9 objects**.

Collecting and Graphing

1. Gather students on the floor and display the large grid. Empty the contents of one bag on the table or floor. You may want to use a set of larger items for better visibility.

2. Ask students how to group and graph the items on the grid; limit them to two or three attributes at a time (e.g., red/not red, big/medium/small). Repeat the game several times until they are familiar with the process.

3. Provide each child with a grid sheet and a small grab bag of items. Challenge students to sort their items into two or three groups and "graph" them on their grids.

4. As the children work, ask them to explain their graphing categories. Can they find other ways to graph items? Can they place all of their items on the grids? What will their graphs look like when finished? How should they label their rows or columns?

5. Show students how to change their object graphs into bar graphs by coloring the squares as they remove each object. They should notice a one-to-one correspondence between items and squares. Encourage students to be creative in how they record their data (e.g., using different colors, shapes, symbols).

6. When finished, students can write or dictate sentences about their data on their papers. They can also create number sentences. (For example, *There are five more green buttons than black buttons. 7 caps + 3 caps + 1 cap = 11 caps.*)

Talking It Over

Talk about the object and symbol graphs. How did the students sort their items? What objects did they graph? What attributes did they use? What totals did they get for each group?

More Grab Bag Fun

1. Help students grasp the concept of a "not" group. Display a set of related items on a tray or in a sorting hoop. Ask why the objects belong in a "family." Place things that don't belong to the chosen family in a second space. Have students look at the items that do not belong and find reasons to exclude them. Also provide them with additional items and ask them if the items belong in the family.

2. Invite students to find and use small classroom manipulatives to make their own fun grab bags for classmates to sort, group, and graph.

3. Students can work in pairs to sort items in their grab bags, then see if their partners can guess their graphing or sorting rules. They can take their grab bags home to "stump" their family members with their rules, or they can prepare their own grab bags at home to sort with their families.

4. Display pairs of items and invite students to find things that are similar and different about the items. Write their comments on a graph titled *Same or Different*. Students can attach objects or drawings of the objects to the graph.

Is Your Hair Curly, Straight, or Wavy?

Materials

- ✔ Large chart paper or poster board
- ✔ Books about hair, such as the following:
  - Erandi's Braids by Antonio Hernández Madrigal (Scholastic, 1999)
  - Hats Off to Hair! by Kay Life (Charlesbridge Publishing, 1995)
  - Uncle Jed's Barbershop by Margaree King Mitchell (Scholastic, 1993)
- ✔ Pictures or photographs of people with assorted hair types
- ✔ Small pieces of paper or plain index cards
- ✔ Art supplies

Hair is a personal feature that interests most youngsters! In this activity, children create a class graph showing who has curly, straight, or wavy hair.

Preparation

- Prepare a large graph from the chart paper or poster board. Add enough columns or rows for all of the hair types in the class.

- Enjoy and discuss hair-related books such as *Erandi's Braids* by Antonio Hernández Madrigal, *Hats Off to Hair!* by Kay Life, and *Uncle Jed's Barbershop* by Margaree King Mitchell.

Collecting and Graphing

1. Share pictures or photographs of people with different hair types. What do students notice? Discuss how hair can vary in length, texture, shape, color, style, and quantity.

2. Ask students to look at their classmates. What do they notice about their hair? Discuss similarities and differences. If necessary, have three volunteers with different kinds of hair stand in front to help the discussion.

3. Tell the class that they will create a graph showing three hair types: curly, straight, and wavy. How can they do this? Do they need to agree on what is meant by *straight, wavy,* and *curly*?

4. Provide students with small pieces of paper or index cards and ask them to draw their own heads, paying special attention to their hair.

5. Gather together and decide how to organize the drawings. Help students place their drawings on the table or floor in columns or rows to form three groups (subsets).

6. Show students the graph and help them label the columns or rows. Transfer their data to the appropriate groups. They can add a title such as *Is Your Hair Curly, Straight, or Wavy?*

7. Display the completed graph for students to share and examine.

Talking It Over

Talk about the graph together. What do the children notice? Which hair type is most common? Least common? What is the shape of the data? Does the graph seem to match what they see in the classroom? What might happen if they surveyed another class? What about in a different season? Would they get the same or different data? Why or why not?

More Hair Fun

1. Challenge students to write or dictate number sentences to describe their data. Display the sentences near the hair graph.

2. Working in groups, students can collect a variety of hair data about their classmates (e.g., color, length, bangs, accessories, parts). They can create graphs to share and display their data.

3. Invite a hairdresser to talk about his or her work and tools—and maybe (with parental permission) give a student a trim. Students can survey where they get their hair cut or how often they have a trim.

4. Students can examine their toys and make graphs about the toys' hair (e.g., curly, straight, wavy, or none). Be sure that they share and discuss their findings with the class.

5. Provide students with magazines and greeting cards and ask them to examine the hairstyles shown. They can cut out pictures, then sort and graph the hairstyles according to different attributes (e.g., short, medium, long).

6. With parental assistance, students can find old photos of their parents and other family members and sort them according to hair type. What do they notice? Whose hair did they inherit? (Be sensitive to stepchildren and adopted or foster children.)

Hats Off to You!

Materials

☑ Large chart paper or poster board

☑ Books about hats, such as the following:
- Aunt Flossie's Hats (and Crab Cakes Later) by Elizabeth Fitzgerald Howard (Clarion, 1991)
- Caps for Sale by Esphyr Slobodkina (Scholastic, 1968)
- The Five Hundred Hats of Bartholomew Cubbins by Dr. Seuss (Random House, 1989)
- Hats, Hats, Hats by Ann Morris (Scholastic, 1989)
- Jennie's Hat by Ezra Jack Keats (HarperCollins, 1966)

☑ Student name cards or portraits

☑ Plain index cards (optional)

☑ Art supplies

Kids love wearing and playing with hats. In this activity, students put their names or portraits on a graph to show how many do or don't wear hats on a particular day. Plan this activity for winter or summertime, when children wear hats for warmth or protection.

Preparation

● Prepare a large two-column graph from the chart paper or poster board. Label the columns *Yes* and *No* and title the graph *Did You Wear a Hat Today?*

● Read and discuss stories about hats such as *Aunt Flossie's Hats (and Crab Cakes Later)* by Elizabeth Fitzgerald Howard, *Caps for Sale* by Esphyr Slobodkina, *The Five Hundred Hats of Bartholomew Cubbins* by Dr. Seuss, *Hats, Hats, Hats* by Ann Morris, and *Jennie's Hat* by Ezra Jack Keats.

Collecting and Graphing

1. Have the prepared graph displayed as students arrive at school. Place their portraits, name cards, or index cards nearby.

2. Invite students to put their "data" (portraits or cards) on the graph as soon as they enter the room. Or, have them draw pictures of themselves with or without their hats on index cards, then tape or glue the pictures in the appropriate columns.

3. Display the completed hat graph for the children to share and examine.

Talking It Over

Discuss the graph together. What does the data show? How do the two groups compare? Did more or fewer students wear hats? Why? What if they did the survey in another class? Would they get similar results? Why or why not? What if they conducted this survey in four months' time? Would they get the same results? Why or why not?

More Hat Fun

1. Bring in a variety of hats (e.g., hard hats, baby bonnets, straw hats, clown hats, party hats, police hats) for the children to explore and graph according to various attributes (e.g., colors, materials, homemade/store bought, new/old, fun/functional). If you work with younger children, invite them to sit around a large graphing mat on the floor (or work in groups) to sort hats into different groups.

2. Celebrate hats and invite students to wear or make interesting hats on "Hat Day." They can sort and graph their hats, caps, and helmets according to everyday or light-hearted categories such as *funny, pretty, messy,* and *crazy.*

3. The class can take a hat walk around the community to survey headgear in places such as a city park or the town center. Talk about where they might find the most hats. What kinds will they see? How should they collect this data? How many hats can they find in one minute? In five minutes? Will this data change later in the year?

Height—How Tall Are You?

Children benefit from collecting data that changes over time. In this "growing" activity, they record their heights on a child-size bar graph at the beginning of the school year—and again at the end—to see how much they've grown!

Materials

- ✔ Height chart or a long piece of butcher paper or craft paper
- ✔ One-inch or two-centimeter square of paper
- ✔ Book or small board
- ✔ Art supplies

Preparation

If necessary, prepare a height wall graph (longer than your tallest student) by marking butcher paper or craft paper with one-inch or two-centimeter squares. Provide a one-inch or two-centimeter column for each child and label inches or centimeters along the vertical axis. To save wall space, do not leave spaces between each student's bar.

Collecting and Graphing

1. Ask students what an inch or a centimeter looks like. How big is it? Can they show it with their fingers? Hold up a one-inch or two-centimeter square of paper for the children to examine.

2. Invite a volunteer to come and stand before the group. Ask the class to estimate how many inches or centimeters tall the child is from head to foot. How can they find out for sure? Does it make sense to use the small paper square? What should they use? Talk about rulers and yardsticks and how they are used to measure many inches or centimeters at once.

3. Show the class the wall graph. What do they notice about it? Talk about the one-inch or two-centimeter squares and numbers.

4. Demonstrate how to measure height correctly by having the volunteer stand against the graph. Place a book or small board on the child's head, have him or her step away, and have another child color in the square that meets the marker.

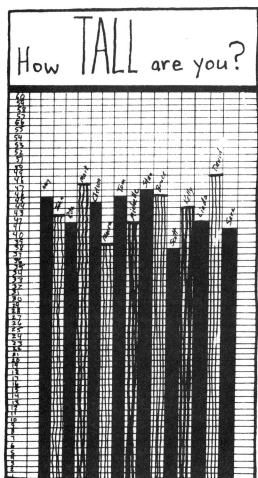

5. Help students count all of the way up the graph from 1 inch or 2 cm to the newly colored square. How tall is the child? Were any estimates close?

6. Invite the volunteer to color the rest of the squares to make a bar. Have the student label the bar with his or her name.

7. Have pairs of students take turns finding, marking, and coloring their heights to make a child-size bar graph.

8. Display the completed height graph all year long for the class to examine and share. They can measure their heights again in the spring and color in the extra squares to show how much they've grown!

Talking It Over

Discuss the graph. Is it what the students expected? Which classmates are the same height? Who is taller or shorter by one inch or two centimeters? By two inches or four centimeters? How many inches or centimeters taller is one child than another? Does any height appear more often than others? What is the range of the data? At the end of the year, talk about how many inches or centimeters the students have grown. How did the data change? Who grew the most?

More Height Fun

1. Have students collect and graph data on the heights of other children in the school to compare with their own class data.

2. Challenge older children to graph the heights of all of their family members and their pets. Talk about how to create a graph with such a wide range of data.

3. Have students make whole-class or individual three-column graphs. In the right-hand columns, they can write names or draw pictures of several things taller than themselves; in the center columns, of several things the same height; and in the left columns, of several shorter things. Students can talk about their data and compare findings.

4. To practice inches or centimeters, students can find and sort items that are longer than, shorter than, and exactly one inch or two centimeters. They can look for objects inside or outside the classroom or use items from teacher-prepared goody bags. The children can draw objects that cannot be picked up or gathered.

5. Enjoy books about growing and changing, such as the following:

   • *Changes* by Marjorie N. Allen and Shelley Rotner (Aladdin Books, 1991)

   • *How Kids Grow* by Jean Marzollo (Cartwheel, 1998)

   • *Inch by Inch* by Leo Lionni (Scholastic, 1960)

   Students can vote on their favorite "growing-up" books, illustrations, covers, or characters. They can also graph responses to specific questions from the literature.

Home, Sweet Home

Materials

☑ Large pieces of chart paper or poster board

☑ Books about bedrooms and bedtime, such as the following:
  • The Going to Bed Book by Sandra Boynton (Simon & Schuster, 1995)
  • The Napping House by Audrey Wood (Harcourt Brace, 1984)
  • Time for Bed by Mem Fox (Harcourt Brace, 1997)

☑ Copy paper

☑ Sticky notes or plain index cards

☑ Art supplies

Almost all children have a home of some kind—and where they live can provide wonderful graphing opportunities. In this activity, students count the number of beds in their homes and place the total number on a bed-shaped graph. If you have homeless students, you may want to forgo this topic. You may also need a plan for children who split their time between two homes.

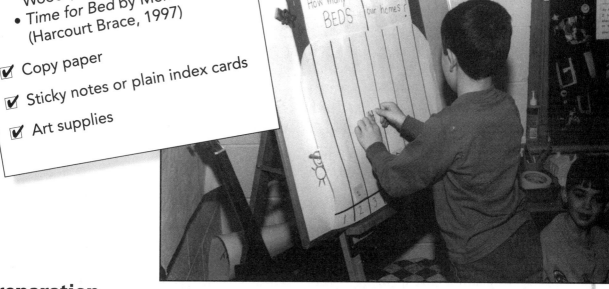

Preparation

● Prepare a large eight-column graph from the chart paper or poster board. Make the graph bed-shaped and add a foot or head board as shown in the photo. Label seven columns with numbers 1–7 and the eighth column *More*.

● Share and discuss "bedtime" books such as *The Going to Bed Book* by Sandra Boynton, *The Napping House* by Audrey Wood, and *Time for Bed* by Mem Fox.

Collecting and Graphing

1. Invite students to talk about their bedrooms. What is special about their rooms? What do they like about them? What color are they? How are they decorated? Do they share a room? What type of bed do they have? How is it decorated?

2. Challenge students to think about the other rooms in their houses and estimate the number of beds.

3. For homework, have students actually count the number of beds in their homes and write the total on index cards.

4. At school, show students the eight-column graph. Have each child write his or her individual bed total on a sticky note. How close were the estimates to the actual totals?

5. Talk about how to group the numbers and invite students to take turns placing their sticky-note data in the appropriate columns. They can also write a title such as *How Many Beds Are in Our Homes?*

6. Invite the class to examine and share the completed graph.

Talking It Over

Discuss the graph together. Is the data easier to understand when it's grouped together this way? Why? What is its shape? What is the range? Did they need the *More* column? Is there one number that comes up most often? Less often? Could this data change over time?

More Home Fun

1. Students can complete simple graphs or Venn diagrams to answer other "homey" questions such as the following:

   • Do you live in a house, apartment, or mobile home?

   • Does your home have one story, two stories, or more?

   • Is your house mostly made of wood, brick, plaster, or something else?

   • How many windows (doors, beds, clocks, telephones) are in your home?

   • Is your home mainly heated with wood, gas, oil, sunlight, or electricity?

   • What color is your home?

   • Was your home built before or after 1990? 1950? 1900?

   • What floor do you live on?

2. Challenge students to construct shelters in the classroom from a variety of materials such as clay, blocks, wood, sticks, cardboard, paper, sugar cubes, plastic bricks, blankets, and sheets. They can also make diorama or shoebox homes, adding tiny furniture and decorations. The children can graph responses to questions about these activities such as *What did you make your house from—sticks, cardboard, paper, sugar cubes, or plastic bricks?* (They can check all appropriate responses.)

3. Enjoy reading home-related books such as the following:

   • *The Big Orange Splot* by Daniel Manus Pinkwater (Scholastic, 1977)

   • *Building a House* by Byron Barton (Trumpet Club, 1981)

   • *Children Just Like Me* by Barnabas and Anabel Kindersley
   (Dorling Kindersley, 1995)

   • *House, House* by Jane Yolen (Marshall Cavendish, 1998)

   • *A House Is a House for Me* by Mary Ann Hoberman (Viking, 1982)

   • *Houses and Homes* by Ann Morris (Lothrop, Lee & Shepard, 1992)

   • *My Painted House, My Friendly Chicken, and Me* by Maya Angelou
   (Crown Publishers, 1994)

   • *This Is My House* by Arthur Dorros (Scholastic, 1992)

   • *The Village of Round and Square Houses* by Ann Grifalconi (Little, Brown, 1986)

   Students can graph their favorite home books, covers, or illustrators. They can also respond to specific questions about the literature, such as *What shape is your house? In what house would you like to live? Which house is most like your place?*

4. Encourage students to do something for a homeless shelter, such as donate toiletries or make cookies. They can graph the progressive total of items collected or made.

5. Older children can work in groups to research different homes around the world (e.g., castles, yurts, log cabins, pueblos, igloos, tepees). They can write their own survey questions for classmates to answer, such as *Who lives in a yurt?*

All Scream for Ice Cream!

Materials

- ☑ Large pieces of chart paper or poster board
- ☑ Copies of Ice Cream Scoops reproducible (page 132)
- ☑ Small paper signs
- ☑ Cardboard or plastic trays (optional)
- ☑ Tubs of four different ice creams
- ☑ Tiny paper cups
- ☑ Tiny plastic spoons
- ☑ Art supplies

Ice cream is always a popular subject. In this delicious activity, students taste different flavors and create a class graph to show their favorites. You may incorporate this activity into a study of food, farms, or fun!

Preparation

- Prepare a large two-column "Question of the Day" graph from the chart paper or poster board (pages 88–89). At the top of the graph, write *Do You Like Ice Cream?* The children can respond yes or no, but expect a lot of positive votes!

- Also prepare a four-column graph labeled with the names of the four ice creams in "cones" at the bottom of the graph.

- Make white copies of the *Ice Cream Scoops* reproducible (one scoop for each child).

- Print the names of the ice cream flavors on paper signs or on the cardboard or plastic trays.

- Check for children with milk allergies.

Collecting and Graphing

1. Talk about ice cream. Why is it so popular? Where does it come from? How is it made? Where do the children get ice cream? How do they like to eat it?

2. With much fanfare, display the four different ice creams, tiny cups and spoons, and paper signs or labeled trays.

3. Volunteers can help spoon the ice cream into the sample cups and display them on the correctly labeled trays or with their paper signs.

4. Invite students to take turns trying the four ice creams and choosing favorite flavors.

5. Show students the labeled graph and ice cream scoops and explain that they are going to graph their favorite flavors. Invite them to predict which will win!

6. Have the children color their scoops to match their favorite flavors and tape or glue their scoops in the appropriate columns. They can also help write a title such as *What's Your Favorite Flavor Ice Cream?*

7. Display the completed ice cream graph for the children to share and examine.

Talking It Over

Discuss the graph. What does it show and tell? How close were the students' predictions? What is the favorite flavor? Are there any surprises? What is the least favorite flavor? Are any flavors liked equally? How could students use this information?

More Ice Cream Fun

1. Working in groups, students can survey other classes to find and compare the most popular ice cream flavors in the school. They can also survey students about different toppings and graph the favorites.

2. Students can ask family members about their favorite flavors and graph the results. They can pool their findings to make a whole-class family-favorites graph. Or, have parents complete this graph at Open House or during conference times and discuss the results the following day in class.

3. With adult assistance, students can read recipes, measure ingredients, and make their own ice cream. They can also graph their responses to specific questions about the activity such as *What ingredients did we use to make our ice cream—milk, sugar, eggs, rice, or salt?* (They can place X's or write their names in all of the correct columns.)

4. Students can survey classmates or family members about their favorite ways to eat ice cream (e.g., cup, cone, shake, pie) and graph the results.

5. Read yummy ice cream books such as the following:

   • *From Milk to Ice Cream* by Ali Mitgutsch (Carolrhoda, 1981)

   • *Ice Cream Larry* by Daniel Pinkwater (Marshall Cavendish, 1999)

   • *Let's Find Out about Ice Cream* by Mary Ebeltoft Reid (Scholastic, 1996)

   • *Simply Delicious!* by Margaret Mahy (Orchard Books, 1999)

   The class can survey and graph favorite ice cream stories, characters, illustrations, or covers. They can also respond to specific questions from the literature, such as *What is the most delicious—ice cream, apple pie, hamburger, candy apple, or fried worms?*

Jack and the Beanstalk

1. Should Jack Have Stolen from the Giant?

Materials

- ☑ Large chart paper or poster board
- ☑ Student name cards, sticky notes, or other ways to record data (e.g., bean seeds, bean pictures)
- ☑ Jack and the Beanstalk (traditional story; different versions available)
- ☑ Art supplies

This popular folk tale is a great springboard for all sorts of wonderful data collecting and graphing activities. In the first thought-provoking idea, students listen to *Jack and the Beanstalk* and decide whether or not it was acceptable for Jack to steal from the giant. In the second "springtime" activity, they plant seeds and use line graphs to chart the seeds' growth.

Preparation

- Prepare a large "Yes or No" graph (pages 124–125) or "Question of the Day" graph (pages 88–89) on the chart paper or poster board. Label the columns with *Yes* and *No* and add the question, *Should Jack have stolen from the giant?*

Collecting and Graphing

1. Read *Jack and the Beanstalk* together and talk about Jack's stealing. What did he take? Why did he steal from the giant? Was it acceptable for him to do this?

2. Explain that students are going to survey their classmates to see how they feel about Jack's stealing. Share ideas about ways to collect and record the data and/or show the prepared "Yes or No" graph.

3. Have the children place their names, sticky notes, or other chosen data markers (e.g., real bean seeds, bean pictures) in the *Yes* and *No* columns, as appropriate.

4. Display the graph near the *Jack and the Beanstalk* book and growing bean plants for the children to share and examine.

Talking It Over

Discuss the graph together. What does it show? Why did the class get these results? Ask volunteers to explain why they said yes or no. Remain impartial so that students feel free to express their opinions.

2. My Own Beanstalk

Materials

- ☑ Copies of Ten-Column/Row Grid reproducible (page 142)
- ☑ Jack and the Beanstalk (traditional story; different versions available)
- ☑ Quick-growing bean seeds (e.g., pole beans) for each student
- ☑ Small flowerpot or milk carton for each student
- ☑ 10-inch (25.4 cm) stakes for each plant
- ☑ Soil
- ☑ Twist ties
- ☑ Interlocking cubes
- ☑ Journals
- ☑ Art supplies

Preparation

● Hand out copies of the *Ten-Column/Row Grid* reproducible. If you work with younger children, label the graphs for a ten-day period before copying to help them chart the growth of their plants.

Collecting and Graphing

1. Read *Jack and the Beanstalk* and show your bean seeds. Are they magic? What might happen if you plant them?

2. Provide each child with a small flowerpot, soil, and a seed. Students can plant and water their bean seeds and predict when they are going to sprout.

3. Each day, younger students can measure their plants with cubes. Help them place cubes on their graphs, then color the same number of squares on their grids to make bar graphs. Or, they can draw dots at the top of the cubes and connect the points to make line plots.

4. Older students can use rulers to measure their plants. Each day, they can plot their plants' growth on their graphs with pencils and connect the points to make line graphs.

5. Monitor students as they measure and record the growth of their plants. Encourage them to keep journals with drawings, descriptions, and other observations about their seedlings.

6. After ten days of school, tape the children's graphs to the wall to compare and discuss the data. They can take their plants home to mature and bear fruit.

Talking It Over

Discuss individual and class data. Ask the class to discuss their results. What patterns did they notice? Can they predict how tall their plants will be? Did all of the plants grow at the same rate and to the same height? Why or why not? (Some children may have watered their beans too much or too little.) Was there a greater difference on Mondays, after two days without data collection?

More Bean Fun

1. Provide students with assorted dried beans (e.g., pinto, soy, lima) to sort and graph according to size, color, and shape. They can glue the beans onto a graph or use stickers to represent their seeds.

2. Students can weigh dried and fresh beans. They can place several seeds in one basket on a balance scale and see how many other objects (e.g., paper clips, peanuts in shells, uncooked pasta, plastic spiders or ants) are needed to balance the scales. Students can graph their results.

3. With parental permission, students can bring favorite vegetables or fruits to class (raw and uncut). They can make an object graph of the most popular ones and group them by color, size, and shape. They may even be able to find their favorite vegetables or fruits in storybooks.

4. Reread different versions of *Jack and the Beanstalk* and have the class graph their favorite versions or illustrations. They can also answer specific questions, such as *Would you rather be Jack or the giant?*

Jump, Frog, Jump!

Materials

☑ Large chart paper or poster board

☑ Books about frogs and jumping, such as the following:
  • Frog and Toad Are Friends by Arnold Lobel (HarperCollins, 1970)
  • Jump, Frog, Jump! by Robert Kalan (Scholastic, 1981)
  • If You Hopped Like a Frog by David M. Schwartz (Scholastic, 1999)

☑ Green construction paper (optional)

☑ Tape measure or other measuring tools

☑ Masking tape

☑ Sticky notes or dots

☑ Frog stickers or stamps

☑ Art supplies

Since it is difficult for most classes to have real frog-jumping contests, let your students be the frogs! In this activity, they take turns jumping as far as they can from a squatting position and then graph their jumping distances.

Preparation

● Prepare a large graph from the chart paper or poster board. Add enough columns for the children's jumping distances and label them accordingly (e.g., *1 foot, 2 feet*).

● Read and dramatize froggy stories such as *Frog and Toad Are Friends* by Arnold Lobel, *Jump, Frog, Jump!* by Robert Kalan, or *If You Hopped Like a Frog* by David M. Schwartz. Students can even make and wear their own froggy masks from green construction-paper headbands.

● Visit a frog pond or other place where students can see frogs jumping—and maybe even catch some.

Collecting and Graphing

1. Squat in front of the class and make a huge leap across the floor, croaking for extra effect! Ask the children how far they think you jumped. (Use their estimates to check their understanding of linear measurement.)

2. Invite students to estimate how far they could go with just one frog jump. They can respond by spreading their hands wide apart, or by describing the distance from one place to another (e.g., *all of the way from your desk to the door*). If students have a concept of units of measurement such as feet or centimeters, they may use these for estimates.

3. Place the tape measure or other measuring tool on the ground and let the class practice jumping like frogs.

4. When ready, students can take turns "frog jumping" along the tape measure. Use pieces of masking tape to mark the places where their feet land first. Write their names on the pieces of tape.

5. Work together to figure out the distance that each child jumps in feet (and possibly inches) or centimeters and help students record their measurements on sticky notes or with dots.

6. Help students place their data in the appropriate columns on the prepared class graph. They can also use sticky dots, frog stickers, or stamps to record their jumps.

7. Display the completed frog-jumping graph for the children to share and examine.

Talking It Over

Discuss the graph. What does it show? What is the shape of the data? What is the range of numbers? How far did most children jump? How can they tell? If the children collected this data last year, would their graph look different? How? Why? How would the data be different if it were collected in ten years?

More Jumping Fun

1. Collect a variety of plastic frogs or other "creepy crawlies" (e.g., spiders, worms, bees) for students to count, sort, and graph.

2. Challenge students to design and make their own paper planes and see if they can throw them farther than the students can jump! They can measure and graph the distances their planes travel.

3. Read other frog-related stories such as the following:

   • *All Eyes on the Pond* by Michael J. Rosen (Hyperion, 1994)

   • *Frog and Toad Together* by Arnold Lobel (HarperCollins, 1971)

   • *The Frog Prince* retold by Edith H. Tarcov (Scholastic, 1974)

   • *Frogs* by Carolyn MacLulich (Scholastic, 1996)

   Students can graph the number of frog pictures in each book or their favorite "froggy" characters, stories, or covers. They can also respond to specific questions about the literature.

Kids—Boys or Girls?

This "boy and girl" activity helps students understand the important connection between real objects and the symbols that represent them. The idea is effective because it uses the most real objects children know … themselves! If you have an all-boy or all-girl class, survey a different characteristic, such as hair color or dimples.

Materials

- ☑ Large chart paper or poster board
- ☑ Student portraits
- ☑ Art supplies

Preparation

Prepare a large two-column graph from the chart paper or poster board.

Collecting and Graphing

1. Invite students to estimate how many girls are in the classroom. What about boys? How could they find out whether there are more girls or boys?

2. Tell students that they will make an object graph to show exactly how many girls and boys are in the class, and that they will use their bodies to make the graph!

3. Talk about how students should arrange themselves so that they can see if there are more girls or boys. Try some ideas and help them line up evenly in rows of boys and girls.

4. Show the large two-column graph and provide students with their portraits. How could they use their photos to make a graph that shows the number of girls and boys? Discuss ideas and try some of them.

5. After students line up their portraits in the two columns, they can help write *Boy* and *Girl* labels and title the graph *How Many Boys and Girls Are in Our Class?*

6. Display the completed graph for students to examine and share.

Talking It Over

Talk about the object and symbol graphs. How did arranging data in two columns or rows make it easier to compare the groups? What about the children who were absent during the activity? Should they be included in the graph? Why? How? Are there more boys or girls in the class? By how many? How close were the children's estimates? How can they use the graph to find out how many children are in the class altogether?

More Boy and Girl Fun

1. Divide the class into two groups according to gender. Pass out interlocking cubes—one color for girls, another for boys. Have students in each group connect their cubes to make "towers." What do they notice? Tape the towers onto paper to make bar graph columns and label the towers. Invite students to explore other ways to represent data (e.g., gluing paper squares in the columns, writing *Bs* and *Gs*, making tally marks).

2. Have two volunteers stand together in front of the class. Invite the class to observe the volunteers carefully to identify things that are the same (e.g., both are girls, both have two arms, both wear socks) or different (e.g., one has glasses, one is taller, one is wearing red). Be sure to keep the observations factual and not subjective (e.g., one is nice, or pretty). Repeat this activity with other pairs of children or adults.

3. Play "Guess Who?". Model how to use the classroom graphs to make up a riddle about a "mystery child" and how to use the process of elimination to identify the person. For example, *This person has a dog, two little brothers, is right-handed, likes purple, and loves peppermint ice cream. Guess who I'm thinking of?* Students can take turns playing the game and sharing their clues with the whole class. Encourage them to keep the identity of the mystery person a secret until everyone has a chance to study the graphs. They may write down the mystery person's name or raise hands to show that they know the answer.

All about Leaves

Materials

- ☑ Someday a Tree by Eve Bunting (Clarion, 1993)
- ☑ Assorted leaves (about 10 for each pair of students)
- ☑ Small plastic or paper bags
- ☑ Pieces of chart paper or poster board (for each pair of students)
- ☑ Plain index cards
- ☑ Art supplies

Young children love this fall activity whether the leaves in their community turn splendid autumn shades or remain green. They can work in pairs to sort different leaves and glue them in place to make real graphs.

Preparation

● Read and discuss *Someday a Tree*—the story of people who try to save a sick, old neighborhood oak tree. Talk about what makes trees so special.

● If a leaf walk is difficult to arrange, bring leaves for the class.

Collecting and Graphing

1. Take students on a "leaf walk" to explore different trees. Point out the leaves, with their assorted shapes and colors. See if the children can name or identify any of the trees.

2. Provide each pair of students with a small plastic or paper bag and have them carefully collect about ten leaves from the ground (or a few from the trees if necessary). The children can store their leaves in their bags.

3. After the "leaf walk," give each pair of students a piece of chart paper or poster board. They can spread their leaves on the paper and study them.

4. Talk about ways to sort the leaves (e.g., size, color, shape, deciduous/evergreen, old/new) and invite each pair to choose how to group their leaves.

5. Help students draw two or more columns or rows on their paper and label them with their sorting rules (e.g., *red, yellow, green*). They can tape or glue their leaves directly onto their graphs and add their own titles.

6. Display the finished leaf graphs and invite students to present and explain their graphs to the class.

Talking It Over

Encourage students to ask questions and make observations. What do they notice about the data? How did most students sort their leaves? Why? Were there fewer or more of one kind of leaf? Why? What if they collected their leaves in winter? Summer? In a different part of town? Record students' observations on index cards and display them with the graphs. (For example, *Jaime and Alyssa graphed by size, just like Tina and me. Most of the leaves we collected are brown. Nobody but us graphed by texture.*)

More Fun with Leaves

1. Enjoy other "leafy" books such as the following:

   • *Aani and the Tree Huggers* by Jeannine Atkins (Lee & Low Books, 1995)

   • *Autumn Leaves* by Ken Robbins (Scholastic, 1998)

   • *Have You Seen Trees?* by Joanne Oppenheim (Scholastic, 1967)

   • *Why Do Leaves Change Color?* by Betsy Maestro (HarperCollins, 1994)

   Students can graph their favorite tree stories, characters, illustrations, or covers. They can also respond to specific questions about the literature.

2. Working at different centers, students can create art projects such as leaf rubbings, leaf prints, and leaf collages. They can preserve their leaves between sheets of ironed wax paper or clear self-adhesive paper and cut them out to make fall mobiles. They can graph their favorite leaf-art activities and talk about their choices.

3. Challenge students to make original real-leaf patterns by gluing leaves in rows (e.g., oak, oak, maple; or big, little, little, little). They can also use rubber leaf stamps to make their designs and color their leaves with crayons to create different arrays. They can display their patterns and ask their classmates tricky questions about their designs.

Left-Handed or Right-Handed?

Materials

- ☑ Long length of chart paper or poster board
- ☑ Copies of *Hands* reproducible (page 131)
- ☑ Blindfolds
- ☑ Skin-toned crayons
- ☑ Art supplies

How many left-handers are in your classroom? What about right-handers, or children who are ambidextrous? In this activity, students place paper hands in the appropriate columns to show their dominances.

Preparation

- ● Prepare a long two-column graph from the chart paper or poster board. Label columns *Left* and *Right*. If some children have not established hand dominance, add a third column labeled *Both* or use a Venn diagram.

- ● Distribute copies of the *Hands* reproducible.

Collecting and Graphing

1. Blindfold a volunteer and give the child an object to feel. How much can he or she tell about it just by feeling? Talk about why touch is important. What do students use their hands for? Make a long list of ideas on the board.

2. Ask students if they use one hand more than the other. Which hands do they use? Do more children use their right hands, or their left hands? How can they collect data about this?

3. Provide students with a left- or right-hand pictogram (or both), depending on their dominance. They can color their "hands" with crayons to match their skin colors and write their names on their work.

4. Talk about how to arrange the hands on the chart (e.g., in two long columns or two clusters). Help students tape their paper hands in the *Left* or *Right* (or *Both*) columns and title the graph *Are You Right- or Left-Handed?*

5. Display the completed hand graph for students to examine and share.

Talking It Over

Discuss the graph together. How many students are right-handed? Left-handed? Both? Why are most people right-handed? What about students' family members? If they made a family survey, what would they find? Can they expect similar results from other classrooms?

More Hand Fun

1. Rather than using pictograms, students can make actual left or right watercolor "hand prints" in the appropriate graph columns.

2. Talk about fingerprints and encourage students to explore their own prints. They can use their handprints and fingerprints to make pictures, patterns, and number sentences for classmates to solve and enjoy.

3. Read and talk about hands and skin tones in books such as the following:

   • *All Kinds of Children* by Norma Simon (Albert Whitman, 1999)

   • *All the Colors of the Earth* by Sheila Hamanaka (Morrow Jr. Books, 1994)

   • *Black Is Brown Is Tan* by Arnold Adoff (HarperCollins, 1992)

   • *Black, White, Just Right!* by Marguerite W. Davol (Albert Whitman, 1993)

   • *My Hands* by Aliki (HarperCollins, 1992)

   • *Why Am I Different?* by Norma Simon (Albert Whitman, 1993)

   • *Words in Our Hands* by Ada B. Litchfield (Albert Whitman, 1980)

   The class can graph their favorite "hand" books, characters, or illustrations. They can also respond to specific questions about the literature.

Macaroni and Cheese, or Spaghetti?

Materials

- ✔ Large chart paper or poster board
- ✔ Strega Nona by Tomie de Paola (Simon & Schuster, 1975)
- ✔ Uncooked spaghetti pieces and macaroni
- ✔ Art supplies

Most children love pasta—and after enjoying a good pasta story, they can create a pasta graph! In this tactile activity, students place pasta pieces in columns to vote for their favorite dish.

Preparation

Prepare a large graph from the chart paper or poster board. Make two or three columns or rows on the graph, depending on whether all of your students like pasta.

Collecting and Graphing

1. Read *Strega Nona*, a delicious old tale retold and illustrated by Tomie de Paola. Discuss pasta. What is it? Where did it first come from? How many kinds of pasta dishes can the children think of? Do they have a favorite?

2. Challenge students: Do they prefer spaghetti, or macaroni and cheese? How can they find out which pasta dish is the most popular in their classroom?

3. Show students the large graph and the uncooked spaghetti or macaroni pieces. Talk about how to show pasta votes on the graph. Students can help label the columns *Spaghetti* and *Macaroni and Cheese*. If some do not like pasta, add a third column labeled *Neither* or *Do Not Like*.

4. Place the graph on the rug or table and ask the children to take turns gluing their preferred pasta in the appropriate columns. Help them line up the pieces so that they are level with each other across the columns.

5. When the pasta is dry, display the completed graph for the class to examine and share.

Talking It Over

Discuss the graph. What do the students notice about the data? Did both types of pasta get the same number of votes? Did more children like one kind of pasta than the other? By how much? Would students get the same data if they asked the class next door? Why or why not? What about the children who don't like pasta?

More Pasta Fun

1. With adult assistance and a pasta machine, students can make pasta from scratch. Or, they can help prepare simple spaghetti and macaroni and cheese dishes from store-bought mixes. They can graph their responses to questions about the ingredients and recipes.

2. Display assorted varieties of uncooked pasta. Invite students to choose and graph their favorite shapes. What do they discover?

3. Students can use a variety of pasta shapes, sizes, and colors to sort, count, graph, and make patterns. They can also string their patterns to form chunky necklaces. Students can help dye pasta for their activities by placing uncooked pasta in jars and adding food coloring and rubbing alcohol. They can shake the jars until the pasta is evenly coated, and spread the pieces out on newspaper to dry.

4. Invite the class to investigate what happens when pasta is cooked. How much does it expand? Older students can write math sentences to describe the expansion. (For example, ½ cup uncooked = 1 cup cooked. The macaroni doubled its size when cooked.)

5. Enjoy other pasta books such as the following:

   • From Wheat to Pasta by Robert Egan (Children's Press, 1997)

   • On Top of Spaghetti by Tom Glazer (Goodyear, 1995)

   • Pasta Factory by Hana Machotka (Houghton Mifflin, 1992)

   The class can discuss their favorite pasta stories and vote on the tastiest illustrations or covers. Students can also respond to specific questions about the literature, such as What do you prefer on top of your pasta—meatballs, cheese, ketchup, or nothing?

Don't Forget Your Mittens!

Whether children live where winters are freezing cold or temperate, they can enjoy simple mitten activities. In this idea, students put their names on a class graph to show how many do and don't wear mittens to school on a particular day.

Materials

☑ Large chart paper or poster board

☑ Student name cards

☑ Assorted mittens

☑ Art supplies

Preparation

● Prepare a large two-column graph from the chart paper or poster board. Make the graph mitten-shaped for fun. Label the columns *Yes* and *No* and title the graph *Did You Wear Mittens to School Today?*

● Plan to begin the day with this activity so that the children find it easier to remember what they wore to school.

Collecting and Graphing

1. Display the graph when students arrive at school. Place their name cards nearby.

2. As students enter the room, they can place their names in the *Yes* or *No* columns of the graph. Students who wear gloves should put their names in the *No* column, since the activity is about mittens.

3. After all children have arrived and "graphed" their data, gather them together to examine the completed graph.

Talking It Over

Discuss the graph. What does it show? If the children had their names in the *No* column, did this mean they had nothing on their hands? Does the graph show who wore gloves and who came bare-handed? How could the children gather that data to make a different graph? What would the graph look like if they collected data in June? Why?

More Mitten Fun

1. Read two popular versions of the old Ukrainian folk tale, *The Mitten*—one retold by Alvin Tresselt (Lothrop, Lee & Shepard, 1964) and the other adapted by Jan Brett (Scholastic, 1989). Help students create a Venn diagram showing similarities and differences in the stories. They can dramatize or graph their favorite versions, illustrations, authors, or covers. They can also respond to specific questions about the story, such as *Which animals were NOT in the mitten—a mouse, a koala, a bird, or a dinosaur?*

2. Challenge students to think about what else crawls into the mitten. They can write and illustrate their ideas for a class big book, individual storybooks, or a bulletin-board display with all kinds of creatures squeezing into a large paper mitten. They can survey their classmates with questions about their new stories.

3. Provide assorted mittens and gloves for students to sort, graph, and order by size, weight, color, pattern, or other attributes.

4. Place a pile of mittens on the floor and see how quickly students can put all of the mates together. Repeat the activity with gloves.

5. Place two snowballs on a table, with one ball inside a mitten. Ask students to predict which snowball will melt more quickly. They can graph their choices and observe the snowballs as they melt to verify their predictions. Students may think that the mitten will warm the snowball and make it melt faster. However, the mitten actually insulates the snow from the warm classroom air and slows down the thaw. Older children can explore why the snowball in the mitten melts more slowly.

6. Students can examine three different mittens and estimate which weighs the most. They can check their estimates by weighing the mittens on a balance scale and using sticky dots to record the heaviest one.

What's Your Name?

Most children enjoy activities about their names! In this two-part "name game," they explore connecting the *concrete* to the *symbolic*. They use cubes and name cards to graph and compare the number of letters in their names. (Older or experienced graphers can omit the cube graph and move on to the symbol format.)

Materials

- ✔ Large chart paper or poster board
- ✔ Sentence strips
- ✔ Tikki Tikki Tembo retold by Arlene Mosel (Scholastic, 1968)
- ✔ Length of butcher paper or craft paper
- ✔ Interlocking cubes
- ✔ Art supplies

Preparation

● Prepare a large graph from the chart paper or poster board. Add nine or more columns.

● Print each child's first name on a sentence strip. (Space the letters so that the children can place an interlocking cube on each letter to make a "name train.")

● Read and discuss *Tikki Tikki Tembo*—a popular fable about why Chinese children have short names.

Collecting and Graphing

1. Talk about names. Where did students get their names? Do they know what their names mean? What else would they like to be called? Do they have long or short names? How many letters are in their names? How could they make a chart to show who has the longest and/or shortest names?

2. Give each student a handful of interlocking cubes and a sentence strip with his or her first name. Ask students to place one cube over each letter in their names. Do they need more cubes? Do they have some left over?

3. After covering their names, students can snap the cubes together to make "name trains." They can count the number of cubes as they work.

4. Place the long length of butcher paper or craft paper in the middle of the floor and ask the class to put their name trains on it. Talk about how to group their names; try some of the suggestions.

5. Help the children group name trains of the same length together and arrange the trains in columns from shortest to longest. They can label the columns with numbers 1–9 and the word *More*, if necessary.

6. Help students replace their name trains on the graph with their name cards. Later, they can remove their cards and print their names in the appropriate columns.

7. Display the completed name graph for the class to examine and share.

Talking It Over

Discuss the graph together. What does it show? What is the shape of the data? What is its range? Is there a name length that is typical? Would students get similar data from another classroom? A different country?

More Name Fun

1. Students can graph their middle and/or last names and compare these graphs with the first chart. Discuss similarities and differences. Older children can make number statements comparing the letters in their names with those in their classmates' names.

2. Regularly survey students to see if they do or don't have a specific letter in their first or last names. Also, challenge older students to rearrange the letters in their names to make new words.

3. Without allowing the class to see, print Tikki's full name on a long strip of adding-machine paper or a sentence strip: *Tikki Tikki Tembo No Sa Rembo Chari Bari Ruchi Pip Peri Pembo.* Review the story of *Tikki Tikki Tembo* and repeat the boy's full name. Ask the children to estimate how many letters are in Tikki's name. Unroll the adding-machine paper or sentence strip with his full name and ask students if they think their estimates are close. Count all of the letters with the class and show them that there are fifty letters in Tikki's name. Talk about where they would place this name on their graph.

4. For homework, students can graph the number of letters in the names of all their family members. They can share their graphs with their classmates.

5. Look for other stories about names, such as the following:

   • *My Name Is Alice* by Jane Bayer (Puffin, 1992)

   • *But Names Will Never Hurt Me* by Bernard Waber (Houghton Mifflin, 1976)

   • *Chrysanthemum* by Kevin Henkes (Greenwillow, 1991)

   The class can also look for interesting names in their books, and graph the trickiest, funniest, or scariest names.

Number Rolling Game

In this clever combination game, students work in pairs to roll number dice and write numerals on their graphs. They can explore probability and practice writing numerals at the same time.

Materials

☑ Large chart paper or poster board

☑ Copies of Six-Column/Row Grid reproducible (page 141)

☑ Number dice or wooden inch cubes, numbered 0–5 or 5–10

☑ Overhead projector

☑ Overhead transparencies

☑ Overhead transparency markers

☑ Large foam or milk-carton number dice (optional)

☑ Art supplies

Preparation

● Prepare a large six-column graph from the chart paper or poster board. Label the columns with numbers 0–5 or 5–10, depending on the numbers you want students to practice.

● Hand out copies of the *Six-Column/Row Grid* reproducible. If you work with young children, write a title and numbers 0–5 or 5–10 in the boxes along the top row.

● Prepare overhead transparencies of one or both grids.

● If using wooden inch cubes, write numbers 0–5 or 5–10 on the faces.

Collecting and Graphing

1. Gather the class around the overhead projector with a transparency grid, markers, and a large die.

2. Ask a volunteer to roll the die. Show how to write the number that comes up (e.g., 4) in the first (bottom) square of the *4* column on the grid.

3. Have another volunteer roll the die and write that number in the appropriate column. Continue writing the numerals from bottom to top until the children fill one of the columns.

4. Tell students they are now going to do the number rolling with partners. Do they think they'll get the same results as seen on the class graph?

5. Provide each pair of students with a die numbered 0–5 or 5-10 and a number-rolling grid. They can take turns making predictions, rolling their dice, and writing the numerals on the grids.

6. Display all of the number-rolling graphs on the wall for the class to examine and compare.

Talking It Over

Discuss the graphs together. What do the students notice about their own data? Did one number come up more often? Hardly at all? Would their graphs look the same if they played the game again? How do their graphs compare with the others? Did all of the students roll the dice the

same number of times? How can they tell? Could they make a graph showing how many times all of the students rolled the dice? What might this graph show?

More Number Rolling Fun

1. Invite students to predict what might happen if they played the game again. After they repeat the game, they can talk about their data. Did they get the same results? Why or why not?

2. Have students repeat the game but ask partners to use different colored pencils or crayons to write their numbers so that they can tell their numbers apart. How do their rolls compare? Can they make a graph of their own rolls?

3. Challenge students to invent their own "Number Rolling" games. They may draw shapes or letters on their dice and see which shapes occur most frequently. They may use two dice and add or subtract the two numbers that come up with each toss. Make sure that the children share and discuss their games and graphs.

How Old Are You?

Age graphs are fairly simple for children to create, and they are good experiences for beginning graphers. In this activity, students place their names (or portraits) on a graph to show their ages. If you leave the graph up all year, they can watch their data change shape as they move their names on their birthdays. You may choose to complete this activity after constructing the birth-date graph (pages 16–18).

Materials

☑ Large chart paper or poster board

☑ Student name cards or portraits

☑ Art supplies

Preparation

For younger children, prepare a large graph from the chart paper or poster board. If your class' age spread is wider, add two columns or more.

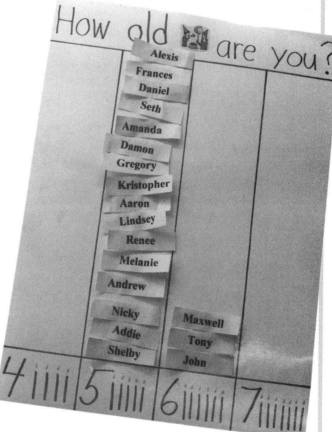

Collecting and Graphing

1. Talk about birthdays and growing older. Ask students if they all share the same age. How can they find out? Explain that they are going to help create a class graph that shows their classmates' ages at the moment. Talk about ways to make this graph.

2. Show students the chart paper or poster board or the prepared two- or three-column graph. Help them label the columns with their ages.

3. Provide students with their name cards or portraits and help them place their data in the appropriate age columns. They should try to keep their data in straight, even columns to make it easier to count and compare the groups.

4. Display the completed age graph for the class to examine and share.

Talking It Over

Discuss the graph. What do students notice about the data? How old are most of the students at the moment? Who is the youngest? Oldest? How can they tell? If they were to leave the graph up all year, would the data change? How? Can they make any other predictions? Students can also refer to the birth-date graph (pages 16–18) to answer some of these questions.

More Age Fun

1. Students can survey family members, including grandparents, to find out their ages and then graph the data to share with classmates.

2. Have students survey the next youngest and oldest grades to find out the range of ages in those classes. They can make a large bar graph showing the age spans of all three grades.

3. Challenge students to explore the numbers that represent their ages. Ask them to give some facts about their numbers. (For example, for 6: Insects have 6 legs, 2 + 4 = 6, 6 is an even number, three school lunches cost $6.) They can also create designs with the appropriate quantity of pattern blocks, paper shapes, or overhead transparency shapes.

One Hundredth Day of School

Materials

- ☑ Books about the one hundredth day of school, such as the following:
  - The 100th Day of School by Angela Shelf Medearis (Cartwheel, 1996)
  - Miss Bindergarten Celebrates the 100th Day of Kindergarten by Joseph Slate (Dutton, 1998)
- ☑ Large jar with a lid
- ☑ One hundred tiny objects (e.g., valentine candies, buttons, shells, coins)
- ☑ Large chart paper or poster board
- ☑ Sticky notes
- ☑ Art supplies

Celebrating the hundredth day of school is becoming a popular classroom activity, and you could probably find more than one hundred ways to enjoy this special day. This list of activities focuses on data collecting and graphing.

Preparation

● Without allowing the class to see, fill a large jar with one hundred tiny objects. Seal contents safely with a lid.

● Read and discuss a story about this special day such as *The 100th Day of School* by Angela Shelf Medearis or *Miss Bindergarten Celebrates the 100th Day of Kindergarten* by Joseph Slate. Talk about why this day is so special. What are some ways to celebrate it?

Collecting and Graphing

1. Display the jar filled with its tiny contents. Invite students to examine it without removing the lid.

2. Challenge students to estimate how many objects are in the jar. They can write their estimates on sticky notes and place them on the chart or board.

3. Talk about ways to group the data (e.g., in columns labeled *1–25, 26–50,* and so on) and how many groups should be used. Students can help draw and label the columns on the chart paper or poster board, and title the graph *How Many Hearts Are in the Jar?* (or other appropriate title).

4. Invite students to place their sticky-note estimates in the appropriate columns and complete the graph.

5. Have students help count out the contents of the jar, using tally marks to track and discover the true number!

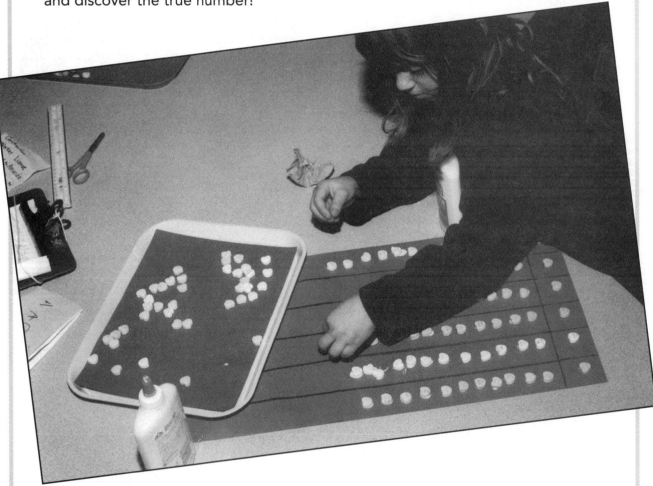

Talking It Over

Examine the graph. Whose estimate was the closest to the actual number? What was the range of estimates? What was the highest or lowest number?

More One Hundredth Fun

1. Have students sort and graph one hundred items (e.g., hearts, plastic animals, colored candies, stickers, stamps) by attributes such as color, shape, or size.

2. Talk about what students can do in one hundred seconds. Working in pairs, they can perform activities that can be counted (e.g., bouncing a ball, making *O*'s) and record their data on a class graph. Talk about why there is such a range of numbers, and why some activities take longer than others.

3. For Open House, students can help prepare a jar that contains more than one hundred tiny items. They can invite their parents to graph their estimates and then check to see who was closest on the following day. Of course, students must keep the real number top secret!

4. Look for other books about big numbers, such as the following:

   • *From One to One Hundred* by Teri Sloat (Dutton, 1991)

   • *The Hundred Dresses* by Eleanor Estes (Harcourt Brace, 1974)

   • *Millions of Cats* by Wanda Gag (Putnam, 1988)

   • *The 329th Friend* by Marjorie Sharmat (Macmillan, 1979)

   • *The Wolf's Chicken Stew* by Keiko Kasza (Putnam, 1987)

   Students can count the items on the pages and graph the data.

Pepperoni or Plain?

Materials

- ☑ Two large paper or cardboard circles, or a large pizza tray and a paper or cardboard circle the size of the tray
- ☑ Two pizzas, one cheese and one pepperoni (optional)
- ☑ Pepperoni and mozzarella cheese (optional)
- ☑ Knife (teacher use only)
- ☑ Napkins (optional)
- ☑ Paper plates (optional)
- ☑ Art supplies

Round foods such as pizza, pancakes, and watermelons are wonderful ways to learn about pie charts or graphs. In this pizzeria activity, children choose their favorite pizzas and color "slices" to make a circle graph of their preferences!

Preparation

Divide one paper or cardboard circle into slices or wedges (one slice per child).

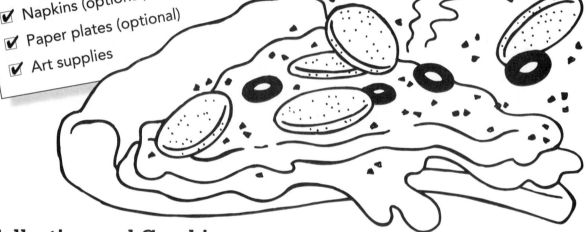

Collecting and Graphing

1. Talk about pizza and favorite ways and places to eat this popular food. If you are not planning a pizza party or to make your own pizza, have a pizza tasting activity by allowing students to sample tiny pieces of pepperoni and mozzarella cheese.

2. Provide students with their own paper "slices" and explain that they are going to create a circle graph to show which type of pizza they prefer—pepperoni or plain.

3. Students can indicate their choices by coloring their pieces to match their favorites. Pepperoni lovers can add brown or red circles to their slices, while those who prefer plain can color their papers a cheesy yellow.

4. Have the children arrange their slices on the round pan or cardboard circle. Talk about the best way to organize the data so that the graph is easy to read.

5. Help students place all of the same types of pizza together and tape or glue their slices to the round pan or cardboard circle.

6. Display the completed pizza pie chart for the children to share and examine.

Talking It Over

Discuss the pie graph together. What do students notice? Do most like the same kind of pizza? How many more like one kind than another? How could they use this information? Can they write a number sentence about the data? (For example, *Three more people like pepperoni. Half the class likes cheese and half likes pepperoni.*)

More Pizza Fun

1. With adult assistance, students can make simple English-muffin pizzas or add toppings to prepared pizza bases. They can graph their topping choices and respond to questions about the ingredients. (For example, *On your pizza, did you use tomato sauce, or ketchup?*)

2. Set up a make-believe pizzeria in a corner of the classroom. Place red-and-white cloths on one or two tables and add pizza trays and colored-paper "pizza slices" and "toppings." Students can count, sort, graph, add, and subtract the pizza pieces and toppings. They can also use real or paper slices to learn about fractions.

3. Make a circular list of round objects such as wheels, cookies, Frisbees®, and marbles. Students can graph their favorite or least favorite round things. They can also weigh assorted round objects on a balance scale and graph the heaviest or lightest items.

4. Show a large round object such as a pumpkin or watermelon. Have students use string to estimate the distance around the object and then measure to see how close they were. The children can make string graphs of their estimates!

5. Plan a pizza party to celebrate a classroom achievement (e.g., total number of books read) and use the data from this activity to order the students' favorite types of pizza.

6. Enjoy pizza books and songs such as the following:

   • *Curious George and the Pizza* (adapted from the film series) edited by Margaret Rey and Alan J. Shalleck (Houghton Mifflin, 1985)

   • *Hold the Anchovies!* by Shelley Rotner and Jill Pemberton Hellums (Orchard Books, 1996)

   • *How Pizza Came to Queens* by Dayal Kaur Khalsa (Clarkson N. Potter, 1989)

   • "I Am a Pizza" from *Ten Carrot Diamond* by Charlotte Diamond (Charlotte Diamond Music, 1985)

   The class can graph the tastiest books, illustrations, or covers. They can also respond to specific questions about the literature.

Celebrating Our Pets

Materials

☑ Books about pets, such as the following:
- *The Best Pet Yet* by Louise Vitellaro Tidd (Scholastic, 1998)
- *Counting on Calico* by Phyllis Limbacher Tildes (Scholastic, 1995)
- *The Day Jimmy's Boa Ate the Wash* by Trinka Hakes Noble (Dial, 1980)
- *Zack's Alligator* by Shirley Mozelle (HarperCollins, 1989)

☑ Large chart paper or poster board

☑ Plain index cards

☑ Art supplies

Animals are always a popular topic, and children love to talk about pets. In this activity, students provide data about their pets to create a class graph.

Preparation

Share and discuss stories about pets, such as *The Best Pet Yet* by Louise Vitellaro, *Counting on Calico* by Phyllis Limbacher, *The Day Jimmy's Boa Ate the Wash* by Trinka Hakes, and *Zack's Alligator* by Shirley Mozelle.

Collecting and Graphing

1. Talk about why people have pets, and how they feel about them. Do all of the children have pets? Do they have the same kinds? How could they find out? How could they collect data to make a class pet graph?

2. Show students the large piece of chart paper, and provide them with index cards. Explain that they are going to make a graph to show which pets they own.

3. Ask students to draw pictures of each type of pet they have, not the number of pets. If a student has three cats, he or she should only draw one cat. Students can write their names on their pictures. Children who do not have pets may make decorative pictures to put above the columns or rows.

4. Decide how to group and attach the animal data to make a graph. Students can help draw and label the columns and rows.

5. Display the completed pet graph along with animal pictures, books, and poems for the class to examine and share.

Talking It Over

Discuss the graph. What does it show? How many different types of pets do the students have? Does anyone have four kinds of pets? Does the graph show how many pets the students have? How could they collect that data?

More Pet Fun

1. Students can work together or in groups to complete simple "Yes or No" graphs about ordinary and extraordinary pets such as hamsters, goldfish, zebras, and whales.

2. Arrange for the class to collect pet data from other classrooms and compare the results. Which class has the most pets? What is the most common or least common pet in the school?

3. Have a "Pet Day" or "Pet Show" at school and invite students to show their pets. They can graph the number and/or type of pets that visit on that day.

4. Read a fun book of math animal riddles, such as *How Many Feet? How Many Tails?* by Marilyn Burns (Scholastic, 1996). Have students make up their own pet riddles, such as *What has five heads, four tails, and ten feet?* Challenge them to think of alternative solutions (e.g., a cat, a bird, two goldfish, and a lizard without its tail). They can compile their pet riddles into class books to display near the graph.

5. Students can sort and graph little plastic pets (or pet pictures) such as fish, birds, snakes, and mice according to attributes such as color, size, and type.

6. Throughout the year, have students use standard and nonstandard measures to collect animal data about different class pets. For example, when baby hamsters are born, students can graph their growth by weighing them in the balance scales. They can also measure and graph their lengths and colors.

7. The class can celebrate pets by raising money or collecting canned or dry food for local animal shelters. They can graph the daily or weekly amounts raised.

8. Invite students to survey the pet books in the library to find the funniest, most common, or favorite pets or animals and graph the results for the book or science corner.

Easy As Pie!

Materials

☑ Two large paper or cardboard circles
☑ Apple and pumpkin pies (optional)
☑ Knife (optional, teacher use only)
☑ Paper plates (optional)
☑ Plastic spoons (optional)
☑ Books about pies, such as the following:
  • How to Make an Apple Pie and See the World by Marjorie Priceman (Knopf, 1994)
  • Where Is the Apple Pie? by Valeri Gorbachev (Philomel, 1999)
☑ Art supplies

There are many ways to enjoy food-related graphs. In this delicious activity—perfect for Thanksgiving—students create a class circle graph to show their preferences for pumpkin or apple pie.

Preparation

● Divide one paper or cardboard circle into slices or wedges (one slice for each child).

● If planning a pie taste test, place apple and pumpkin pies on plates and prepare small slices for each student.

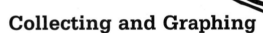

Collecting and Graphing

1. Read a mouth-watering pie story together, such as *How to Make an Apple Pie and See the World* by Marjorie Priceman or *Where Is the Apple Pie?* by Valeri Gorbachev. Younger children may also dramatize the traditional pie rhyme "The Three Little Kittens."

2. Talk about all sorts of delicious pies and invite students to choose between two favorites: pumpkin and apple. If possible, have a pie taste test and offer small slices to help the children choose.

3. Show students the large paper or cardboard circle and provide them with individual paper "slices." Talk about how to record their pie choices. Should they use different colors? Should they write letters or words on their slices?

4. After students decorate their "pieces of pie," decide how to arrange the slices on the graph. Should they group the pie types together? Why?

5. Students can take turns gluing their slices on the large circle graph in the agreed upon order.

6. Display the completed pie graph for the class to examine and share.

Talking It Over

Discuss the graph. What does it show? Is it easy to compare the two groups? How many students prefer apple? Pumpkin? Which pie do most or the fewest students prefer? Why? (Older students may discuss the data in terms of fractions.)

More Pie Fun

1. With adult assistance, students can bake pies. Each group can be responsible for making its preferred dessert—apple or pumpkin pie. If you work with older students, you may encourage them to help plan, buy ingredients, and write out the recipes. They can also graph simple responses to questions about their pie-baking, such as *Which ingredients did we use in our apple pie—flour, milk, eggs, or pepper?* (Students can choose all appropriate responses.)

2. Students can list as many interesting pies and other wonderful round desserts (e.g., chocolate cakes, tarts, cheesecakes) as they can imagine. They can choose three or four of these and survey their classmates or family members to find their favorites. They can also graph the desserts they'd like to have for supper or a party or to give to their parents.

3. Older students can look through magazines or newspapers to find examples of real-life pie charts. Discuss these graphs together.

4. Students can search the library for "sweet" books such as the following:

   • *The Biggest Birthday Cake in the World* by Elizabeth Spurr (Harcourt Brace, 1991)

   • *The Giant Jam Sandwich* by John Vernon Lord and Jane Burroway (Houghton Mifflin, 1987)

   • *The High Rise Glorious Skittle Skat Roarious Sky Pie Angel Food Cake* by Nancy Willard (Harcourt Brace, 1990)

   • *Pancakes for Breakfast* by Tomie de Paola (Harcourt Brace, 1978)

   • *Thunder Cake* by Patricia Polacco (Putnam, 1990)

   The class can graph the most delicious or funniest stories or illustrations. They can also answer specific questions about the literature, such as *Which do you prefer for breakfast—oatmeal, pancakes, French toast, or waffles?*

What's in Your Pocket?

Materials

☑ Books about pockets, such as the following:
- Katy No-Pocket by Emmy Payne (Houghton Mifflin, 1973)
- A Pocket for Corduroy by Don Freeman (Viking, 1978)
- What's in My Pocket? by Rozanne Lanczak Williams (Creative Teaching Press, 1994)

☑ Outfit with many pockets

☑ Large chart paper or poster board

☑ Sticky notes or plain index cards

☑ Art supplies

Pockets hold special appeal for children—perhaps because they can use them to keep special treasures secret and safe. In this fun-filled activity, students count their pockets and combine their data with classmates' to create a class pocket graph.

Preparation

● Read and discuss stories about pockets such as *Katy No-Pocket* by Emmy Payne, *A Pocket for Corduroy* by Don Freeman, and *What's in My Pocket?* by Rozanne Lanczak Williams.

● Wear an outfit with lots of pockets. You may even like to pull some interesting things from your pockets!

Collecting and Graphing

1. Talk about pockets. Where are pockets found? Why do people have them? What do they carry in their pockets?

2. Display the chart paper or poster board and tell students that they will make a class "pocket" graph. Provide them with sticky notes or plain index cards.

3. Without counting, have each student estimate how many pockets he or she is wearing. You may have to ask them to keep their hands on their knees for this part of the activity.

4. Students can write their estimates on the board and then count their pockets. Partners can check the numbers and write totals on sticky notes or index cards.

5. Ask how many pockets there might be in the classroom today. Can students give a quick estimate based on what they know so far? How can they collect the data to find an exact answer?

6. Have students spread their data or cards on the floor or stick them to the wall. Talk about how to group the numbers in order from smallest to greatest.

7. Help students place their data on the graph and label the rows or columns. They can also add a title such as *How Many Pockets Are There in Our Classroom?*

8. Display the pocket graph for students to examine and share.

Talking It Over

Discuss the graph together. What do the students notice? What is the range of numbers? Are there any children without pockets? How can the students find out how many pockets there are altogether? Discuss and try several strategies for adding up the numbers. Will the students get the same data tomorrow? From the class next door? In a different season?

More Pocket Fun

1. Play "What's in My Pocket?" One child hides something in his or her pocket, and classmates ask "yes" or "no" questions to guess the mystery item.

2. Invite students to find where their pockets are on their clothes—on their tops (shirts), bottoms (pants, skirts), or both. They can make a column graph and a Venn diagram to show their pocket locations. Talk about presenting the same data in two different ways. What did the class discover?

3. Make a class *In My Pocket …* book by sewing or gluing fabric pockets on pages for each child. Students can hide things in their "pockets" and write or dictate sentences about their secret objects.

3. Prepare memory and matching games from a large pocket chart or wall hanging. For example, print a numeral or letter on each pocket and provide small objects for students to match and place inside the correct pockets.

Questions, Questions, Questions!

There are so many opportunities for graphing that students can actually do a daily graph! One simple idea is to include a "Question of the Day" in your daily routine. These graphs can include "Yes or No" (pages 124–125) and "Would You Rather...?" formats. You can make daily questions that relate to assorted curriculum topics, such as *Do you know what an island is?* and *Would you rather live where there is lots of snow or no snow?*

Materials

- ☑ Large pieces of chart paper or poster board
- ☑ Laminating film
- ☑ Student name cards, portraits, sticky notes, or clothespins (page 11)
- ☑ Art supplies

Preparation

- Prepare several two- or three-column or row graphs from chart paper or poster board. Title the graphs *Would You Rather...?* Leave spaces to finish the questions each time you use them.

- Laminate the graphs so that you can easily remove and replace labels and data.

- Before students arrive at school, write a "Question of the Day" on one of your graphs. For example, ask whether students would rather
  — eat a hamburger or a pizza
  — be a cat or a dog
  — fly an airplane or go deep-sea diving
  — visit the past or the future
  — be a shark or a wolf
  — stay a kid forever or be a grown-up
  — be able to turn invisible or fly
  — be an astronaut or a movie star
  — watch TV, read a book, or play outside

- Label the columns with answers and other options (e.g., *Yes, No, Neither, None*).

Collecting and Graphing

1. Display the day's graph and place students' name cards, portraits, clothespins, or sticky notes nearby.

2. As students arrive, they can place their name cards, portraits, clothespins, or sticky notes in or on the columns of their choice. Encourage students to read and answer these questions independently or with assistance from their classmates.

3. After the students have responded, they can examine and share the completed graph.

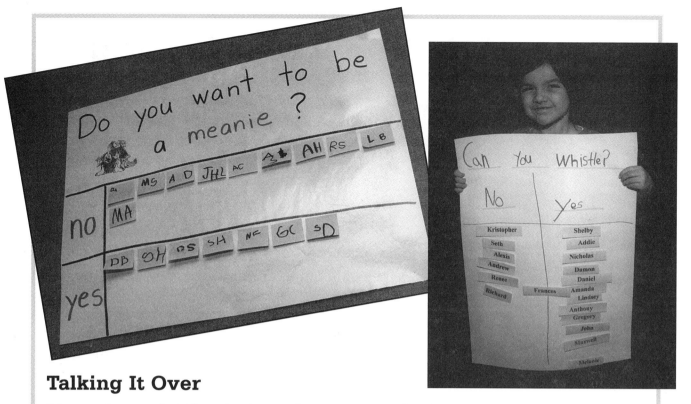

Talking It Over

Discuss the graph. What do the students notice? Why did they get these results? Would the data change if they surveyed another class, or children in another town? Was it hard to make the choice? Do they think their opinions will ever change? Make sure that students realize that it is OK for them to have different opinions about the questions.

More Daily Question Fun

1. As an alternative, write the "Question of the Day" on a small wipe-off board and keep it near the daily graph.

2. Read about all sorts of options in *Would You Rather…* by John Burningham (T. Y. Crowell, 1978). Students can select one or more of these ideas and make their own surveys for their classmates or children from other classrooms.

3. Rather than use a prepared class graph, provide the children with copies of the *Survey* reproducible (page 133). If you work with younger children, add a question and column headings before copying. Students can work in small groups to survey their classmates or family members about a daily question or topic. They can use their surveys to make individual or group graphs to share with the class.

4. Use "Question of the Day" graphs to reinforce specific skills. For example, write two or three math problems at the top of each column and solve each correctly or incorrectly (e.g., *6 – 5 = 1, 8 – 3 = 5, 7 – 2 = 3*). Ask students to examine each problem and write their names beneath those that are solved correctly.

5. Use Venn diagrams when daily questions may have overlapping answers, such as *Do you have a bird or a cat?*

Is It Raining Today?

Whether you live where rain is a frequent, dreary visitor or its appearance is a rare and welcome event, rainy-day activities can provide many opportunities for learning. In the first weather idea, students record the number of days that it rains or doesn't rain. In the second activity, students study and measure puddles before the pools disappear!

1. How Many Days Has It Rained?

Materials

- ☑ Large chart paper or poster board
- ☑ Art supplies

Preparation

● Prepare a large two-column graph from the chart paper or poster board. Add horizontal grid lines to make it easier to count the days. (Allow at least 30 lines if keeping the graph for a month.) Label the columns *Rain* and *No Rain*.

● Go for a rain walk together. Students can look at puddles (jumping in them if dressed properly), study the raindrops, taste the rain, and watch the water swirl down gutters.

Collecting and Graphing

1. During a rainy period, display the graph and explain that your class is going to keep a rain graph for the next month. Decide together when to record the data (e.g., on the same day or the next), as rain can occur later in the day when students are no longer at school.

2. Have the class color a square in the *Rain* or *No Rain* columns every day. Each Monday, they can discuss the weekend's weather and update the graph accordingly.

3. The class can collect data for a month or the whole school year.

Talking It Over

Regularly examine and analyze the data. Did the students choose the best time to collect their data? For how many days did it rain? Were there more rainy days or dry ones? When were the "rainiest" days? How could the class show this data? How can they tell if the dry days were cloudy or sunny? How could they show this data?

1. Rain Puddle Graph

Materials

- ☑ Large chart paper or poster board
- ☑ Standard or nonstandard measuring tools
- ☑ Art supplies

Preparation

● Prepare a large graph from the chart paper or poster board. Add enough columns to make the graph last for several days or for as long as the puddle exists.

● Help the children learn about evaporation. Keep a dish of water in the classroom and have the class watch the amount of water in it gradually decrease. Talk about where the water goes.

Collecting and Graphing

1. After a rainstorm, students can examine a large puddle and predict what will happen to it. Young children may think that all of the water will soak into the ground and not realize that some of it will evaporate.

2. Show students the graph and explain that they are going to measure the width of the puddle each day. They can use standard or nonstandard tools to make their measurements.

3. Help students measure and graph their data each day until the puddle has disappeared.

4. Display the completed puddle graph for the class to examine and share.

Talking It Over

Discuss the graph. What does it show? Did the puddle shrink quickly or slowly? Why? How long before the puddle disappeared? How did the puddle change its shape? What conditions can influence the size of a puddle (e.g., temperature, location, additional rain)?

© Fearon Teacher Aids FE111030

More Rainy Day Fun

1. Students can use media resources (e.g., newspapers, almanacs, Web sites) to collect rain data from different parts of the country. They can graph the data and compare rainfall in these places with that in their own community.

2. Have students create their own rain gauges to measure the daily rainfall. They can record their results and decide how to plot the weekend's rain. They can even analyze weather patterns and make predictions!

3. Students can conduct their own rainy-day surveys with simple questions such as the following:

   • Did you wear rain boots today?

   • Did you wear a raincoat to school?

   • Did you bring an umbrella to school today?

   • Did you jump in a mud puddle today?

   • Do you think we will have recess?

   • Do you think we will see a rainbow today?

   • Do you think tomorrow will be rainy or sunny?

4. Students can paint rainy watercolor pictures and then graph their favorite rain activities.

5. Sing rainy-day songs and read rainy-day books, such as the following:

   • *Cloudy with a Chance of Meatballs* by Judi Barrett (Scholastic, 1978)

   • "Itsy Bitsy Spider" (traditional)

   • *Listen to the Rain* by Bill Martin Jr. and John Archambault (Henry Holt, 1988)

   • *Rain* by Robert Kalan (Greenwillow, 1978)

   • "Rain, Rain, Go Away" (traditional)

The class can accompany the songs and stories with rain, wind, and thunder noises made with handmade instruments. They can also graph their favorite rainy songs or books and answer specific questions about the literature or music.

Ready for Recess!

Just about everyone loves recess! In this "playful" activity, students create a class graph to show their favorite recess activities.

Materials

- ✔ Large piece of chart paper or poster board
- ✔ Copies of *Survey* reproducible (page 133)
- ✔ Small pieces of paper or plain index cards
- ✔ Class lists
- ✔ Art supplies

Preparation

● Prepare a large graph from the chart paper or poster board. Add five to eight columns or rows to accommodate recess activities.

● For older children, hand out copies of the *Survey* reproducible.

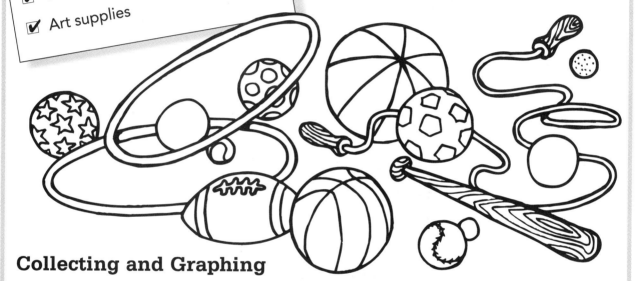

Collecting and Graphing

1. Talk about recess. Why do children like it? What kinds of things do they like to do? Make a list of activities (e.g., jump rope, play hopscotch, climb, play tag, swing, play in the sand, run, shoot hoops, play soccer).

2. Explain that students are going to make a class graph of their favorite recess activities. Decide on five to eight of the ideas and ask them to predict the most popular activity.

3. Young children can draw a favorite recess activity on paper or index cards. They can help label the columns or rows on the graph and place their pictures in the appropriate sections.

4. Older children can work in groups and plan the best way to survey classmates about their favorite activities (e.g., working in groups, writing tally marks next to the choices on their survey sheets). They can transfer the data to the class graph, using X's, sticky notes, or stickers.

5. Display the completed recess graph for the class to examine and share.

 © Fearon Teacher Aids FE111030

Talking It Over

Discuss the graph. What do the students notice? Did they expect the results? Why are certain activities more popular than others? If they did the graph in a different season, would they get the same results? Why or why not? What are the favorite recess activities of the higher or lower grades? What about children in other countries such as Australia or Japan? How could they find out what these children like to play?

More Recess Fun

1. Display a "Yes or No" graph and survey the class with the question *Do you like recess?* Most children will say *yes*. If some respond *no*, they may have issues that need to be addressed.

2. Have students make a list of summer, winter, fall, or spring recess activities. They can survey their classmates to find the most popular ways to spend recess during two of these seasons and graph the results. They can also make a Venn diagram to compare the data. What do they notice? Are there any games that are the same in both seasons? Why or why not?

3. Older children can research other countries to find out the games children play there. They can compare these activities with those they play at recess time.

4. Students can survey their parents to find out their favorite games when they were young. They can pool their data to make a class graph. Or, parents may respond when they visit the classroom for Open House or parent conferences. Talk about the data and how it compares with the children's own recess graph.

5. Survey the class to find out their favorite games or ways to relax at home. Compile this data into a class graph and compare the information with the recess graph.

What's That Shape?

1. What's Your Favorite Shape?

Materials

☑ Assorted blocks (e.g., shape, attribute, pattern)

☑ Geometrical solids (optional)

☑ Large chart paper or poster board

☑ Pieces of paper or small die-cut paper shapes

☑ Art supplies

Shapes are perfect graphing elements because they have distinct attributes. And when you add thickness, color, and size, students have even more ways to graph! In the first activity, children make a class graph showing their favorite geometric shapes. In the second, more challenging lesson, they create pattern-block designs and graph the number of shapes.

Preparation

Provide time for students to become familiar with the names and attributes of shapes through exploratory play. Help them sort the manipulatives into different categories such as shape, color, size, and thickness.

Collecting and Graphing

1. Display assorted blocks and/or geometrical solids. Talk about the shapes and invite the children to secretly choose their favorites.

2. Show students the chart paper or poster board, and provide them with pieces of paper or die-cut shapes. Have each child draw a favorite shape or color one of the die-cuts.

3. Gather students together with their data. Talk about ways to organize shapes to make a graph. Try some of their ideas.

4. Help students place data in columns or rows on the paper according to shapes. They can also help make lines and labels for the columns or rows and add a title.

5. Display the shape graph for the class to examine and share.

Talking It Over

Discuss the graph. What does it show? What is the favorite shape? By how much? What is the least favorite? By how much? How many more or fewer students like one shape than another? Why did they get these results?

1. Graph Your Shape Designs

Materials

- ☑ Copies of Four-, Five-, or Six-Column/Row Grid reproducibles (pages 139–141)
- ☑ Large chart paper or poster board
- ☑ Pattern blocks, 7–12 per student
- ☑ Transparent pattern-block shapes (optional)
- ☑ Overhead projector
- ☑ Work mats
- ☑ Art supplies

Preparation

- Hand out copies of a *Four-, Five-,* or *Six-Column/Row Grid* reproducible. Use the simpler grids for younger children. Before copying, customize the graphs by drawing a shape in each box along the top row.

- Make an enlarged copy of the chosen grid on chart paper.

- Take the children on a class "shape walk" and hunt for shapes in the environment.

Collecting and Graphing

1. As the class watches, make a design out of ten pattern blocks or use transparent pattern-block shapes on the overhead projector.

2. Show the enlarged grid and demonstrate how to "transfer" your design. Count the number of each shape and color the corresponding number of boxes on the grid. For example, if you used three triangles, color three spaces in the triangle row.

3. Provide students with blocks, grids, and work mats with which to create their own designs or pictures.

4. Help students transfer their patterns onto their grids by coloring the squares in the appropriate rows. They can use crayons or markers to match their blocks.

5. Students can name their patterns and write or dictate comments about their data on their papers.

6. Display the completed shape graphs for the class to examine and share.

Talking It Over

Discuss the graphs. What do the students notice? Are some shapes more popular than others? Are some less popular? Do some students have the same data but different designs? How is that possible?

More Shape Fun

1. Challenge students to make number sentences to go with their data. They can share their sentences with classmates.

2. Use hoops or jump ropes to make two separate circles on the rug. Display six blocks for the class to sort into two groups: *red* and *thick*. Hold up a block that is both red and thick. Ask where this block should go. What should they do with it? Help students discover that the block cannot go in either because it needs to be in both. They can create a third space by moving the circles so that they overlap. Continue sorting, placing blocks in the red, thick, and thick and red groups. Introduce a block that does not belong to any of the groups (e.g., a thin, blue block). Help students realize that there is a fourth choice—*neither*—and that they can put data outside the circles.

3. Ask students to bring in snack foods with various shapes (e.g., stick and curled pretzels, fish crackers, square crackers). Provide each pair of children with yarn or plastic circles and handfuls of snacks to sort and graph by various attributes (e.g., shape, size, color, thickness, number of sides). They can also use copies of the *Venn Diagram* reproducible (page 136) to sort their snack foods.

4. Students can look for shapes in books such as the following:

   • *First Shapes* by Ivan and Jane Clark Chermayeff (Abrams, 1991)

   • *Grandfather Tang's Story* by Ann Tompert (Crown Publishers, 1990)

   • *The Maid, the Mouse, and the Odd-Shaped House* by Paul O. Zelinsky (Putnam, 1981)

   • *Pezzettino* by Leo Lionni (Pantheon, 1975)

   The class can count and graph the shapes that appear most frequently in the books.

Who Made Your Shirt?

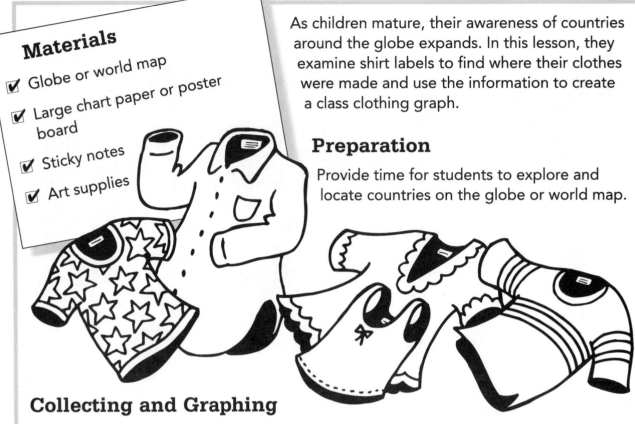

Materials

☑ Globe or world map

☑ Large chart paper or poster board

☑ Sticky notes

☑ Art supplies

As children mature, their awareness of countries around the globe expands. In this lesson, they examine shirt labels to find where their clothes were made and use the information to create a class clothing graph.

Preparation

Provide time for students to explore and locate countries on the globe or world map.

Collecting and Graphing

1. Ask students if they know where their clothes came from. Are most of their clothes made in this country, or imported from other places? How can they find out?

2. Tell students that they will work together to create a graph about where their shirts were made. How can they gather and record the information? Do they know where their shirts were made? Some will think of looking at collar labels. If not, suggest doing so. Have two volunteers stand as you read their shirt labels to the group. If someone has a dress or a shirt without a label, have students decide how to show that information on the graph.

3. Working in pairs, have students read each others' shirt labels to find where the shirts came from and write the names of the countries on sticky notes.

4. Ask one volunteer at a time to tell where his or her shirt was made. As that student places a sticky note on the chart paper or poster board, other students with clothing from the same country can add notes to form a list. Repeat this process until all the children have placed their data on the graph.

5. Discuss how to better organize the sticky-note data on the paper by drawing columns and adding labels and a title.

6. Display the completed shirt graph for the class to examine and share.

Talking It Over

Discuss the graph. What do the students notice? Were more shirts made in this country than imported? If the class collects the data tomorrow, will the graph change? Why or why not? What would happen to the graph if data was collected from all of the children in the school?

Whole School Survey on Where Our Shirts Are Made - 10/23/01

More Shirt Fun

1. Survey the shirts worn by children in other grades to make a multiple-grade graph showing how many shirts were made in this country, and how many were imported. Display the graphs and share and examine the data.

2. Students can bring shirts from home or use themselves and the tops they are wearing to make object or symbol graphs. They can sort and graph their shirts according to attributes such as color, size, collar/no collar, words/no words, long/short sleeves, and the number of pockets and buttons. They can also survey the shirts worn by younger or older classes and graph the data according to chosen attributes. Encourage students to talk about similarities and differences in the graphs.

3. Display a large map of the world. Students can use stickers or pieces of yarn to indicate the countries where their shirts originated. They may use resource books and the Internet to research these places. If you work with older children, encourage them to find statistics about these countries (e.g., population, area, rainfall, average wage, average lifespan) and make graphs comparing these places with their own country. For added challenge, students can try to find out who made their shirts. How much were laborers paid? How did the shirts get into this country?

4. Working in pairs, students can choose a favorite book and survey and count the different articles of clothing illustrated. They can graph and share their findings with the class. Discuss why some books depict more items of clothing than others. (For example, some books have characters who wear clothes, and others, such as nature books, do not.)

Shoes, Sneakers, Socks, and Slippers!

Materials

- ☑ Assorted shoes, boots, and slippers
- ☑ Large chart paper or poster board
- ☑ Graphing mat or long roll of butcher paper
- ☑ Plain index cards (optional)
- ☑ Art supplies

In this popular footwear activity, students enjoy using their shoes to make object graphs.

Preparation

Display assorted shoes, boots, and slippers for students to examine and match. Or, see how quickly volunteers can find their shoes in a central pile.

Collecting and Graphing

1. Select two shoes from different pairs and talk about what is similar and different about them.

2. Have students examine their own shoes and talk about ways they could be sorted (e.g., laces/no laces, buckle/no buckle). Write their ideas on chart paper and decide on a sorting rule together.

3. After students group their shoes, talk about ways to organize them so that the class can tell how many shoes are in each section. Try out some of the students' suggestions.

4. Place a graphing mat or roll of paper on the ground. Explain that students are going to place their shoes in rows or columns across or down the paper. They must let each category have its own space.

5. Have each child take a turn going around the graph and placing one of his or her shoes where he or she thinks it belongs.

6. When finished, students can help make labels on the graph or on index cards for each row or column. They can also add a title such as *First-Grade Shoes*.

Talking It Over

Ask students what they notice about the groups of shoes. Are there more of one kind? Why? How many more are there of one type than another?

More Shoe Fun

1. Students can survey their family members to see what shoes they are wearing or wore today. They can pool information to make a class graph about family shoes.

2. See if students can find out their shoe sizes. Do all of their shoes have the same size? What about their family members? What's the biggest size they can find? Students can make a graph of their classmates' or family members' shoe sizes.

3. Students can time how long it takes them to put on their shoes and tie their laces. They can make a class graph of the results!

4. Have students bring clean, old socks to school to sort and graph according to size and color. They can also see how quickly they can find matching socks!

5. Enjoy reading different versions of *Cinderella* together. Discuss what the stories have in common and what differs. Older children can help make a Venn diagram to compare versions.

6. Read other books about shoes and socks such as the following:

   • *New Shoes for Silvia* by Johanna Hurwitz (Scholastic, 1993)

   • *New Shoes, Red Shoes* by Susan Rollings (Orchard Books, 2000)

   • *A Pair of Socks* by Stuart J. Murphy (Scholastic, 1996)

   • *Whose Shoe?* by Margaret Miller (Greenwillow, 1991)

   The class can graph their favorite shoe or sock books, covers, or illustrators or count to find the books with the most shoes and socks. They can also make their graphs in the shapes of boots or shoes!

Take Me to School!

Materials

☑ Large chart paper or poster board

☑ Copies of Take Me to School reproducible (page 134)

☑ Books about traveling, such as the following:
  - Mr. Gumpy's Outing by John Burningham (Macmillan, 1971)
  - School Bus by Donald Crews (Greenwillow, 1984)
  - This Is the Way We Go to School by Edith Baer (Scholastic, 1990)

☑ Student name cards

☑ Art paper

☑ Art supplies

Planes, trains, and automobiles—so many class activities relate to transportation! In this activity, students place their names on a class graph to show how they came to school that morning.

Preparation

● Prepare a large graph from the chart paper or poster board. Make the graph bus-shaped for fun! Draw and label enough columns or rows to accommodate the different modes of transportation used by your students. Title the graph *How Did You Come to School Today?*

● If using pictograms, hand out copies of the *Take Me to School* reproducible.

Collecting and Graphing

1. Read about going places in *Mr. Gumpy's Outing* by John Burningham, *School Bus* by Donald Crews, and *This Is the Way We Go to School* by Edith Baer. What do these books have in common?

2. Ask students how they came to school today. Did they all come the same way? Why or why not? How could they create a graph to show how they came to school?

3. Show the prepared graph and transportation pictograms. Invite students to choose pictures that show how they came to school that day (or provide the class with art paper to draw their own pictures).

4. Students can color their pictures, print their names on their artwork, and place their data in the appropriate graph columns.

5. Display the completed transportation graph for students to examine and share.

Talking It Over

Discuss the graph. What does it show? How did most children come to school? Why did they get these results? Will they get the same data tomorrow? What about in a different season? Ask specific questions to help students think critically about the data, such as *Why didn't anyone ride a bike today?* (Perhaps it is raining.)

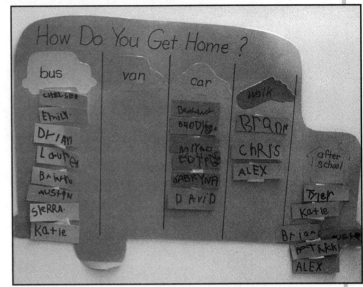

More Transportation Fun

1. Later in the day, change the graph (or make a new one) to show how students get home. Compare the data and discuss why there are some differences.

2. Arrange for students to go into other classrooms to collect data and make an all-school transportation graph about ways children come to school.

3. For fun, ask silly questions such as *How would you rather come to school tomorrow—on the back of a rhinoceros, in the coils of a boa constrictor, or on the wings of a bumblebee?* Students can graph and illustrate responses.

4. Have students survey classmates or family members about types of transportation they have taken or would like to take. Options may include airplanes, hot air balloons, trolley cars, ferry boats, helicopters, ski lifts, and camels.

5. Students can graph sets of vehicles (e.g., tricycles, skateboards, buses) by number of wheels or where they travel (land, sea, air).

6. Have students work in groups to survey and graph transportation preferences. Have them answer questions such as *Would you rather sail a boat, or ride a horse? Fly in the space shuttle, or ride in a submarine?* Display the graphs and talk about the data.

7. Students can count and graph how many cars (and other types of vehicles) drive past the school in five minutes. What about at different times of day? What do they discover?

8. Invite the class to find as many books, songs, and poems as they can that mention transportation. They can sort the books into categories to discover how often different modes of transportation are mentioned.

Have You Lost a Tooth?

Young children are always losing baby teeth, so they usually enjoy tooth-related activities. In this activity, students create a class graph showing how many teeth they have lost. Over time, they can watch the data change shape as classmates move their "teeth" to different columns. You may include this graph in a unit about dental health.

Materials

☑ Large chart paper or poster board

☑ Copies of Teeth reproducible (page 135)

☑ Books about teeth, such as the following:
  - How Many Teeth? by Paul Showers (HarperCollins, 1991)
  - Little Rabbit's Loose Tooth by Lucy Bate (Scholastic, 1975)
  - My Tooth Is Loose! by Martin Silverman (Puffin, 1992)

☑ Hand mirrors (optional)

☑ Art supplies

Preparation

● Prepare a large graph from the chart paper or poster board. Add enough columns for the number of teeth your students may have lost, depending on the age group.

● Hand out copies of the Teeth reproducible.

● Read a story about losing teeth, such as How Many Teeth? by Paul Showers, Little Rabbit's Loose Tooth by Lucy Bate, or My Tooth Is Loose! by Martin Silverman.

● If very young children have not lost any teeth, use a simple "Yes or No" graph with the question, Have you lost a tooth yet? Don't imply that everyone should have lost a tooth.

● Invite a dental health professional to visit and talk about proper dental care.

Collecting and Graphing

1. Discuss teeth. Why do children have teeth? Were they born with them? Why do teeth come out? How should they take care of their teeth? Do other animals have teeth?

2. Ask students how many teeth they have lost and how they could collect that data for a graph. Some may need to look in mirrors, feel their teeth, and do some counting to figure out the number. If older children have trouble remembering, they can make estimates or ask their parents for information.

3. Provide each student with a paper tooth. Have students write their names and the number of teeth they have lost on their paper teeth.

4. Display the graph and talk about how to organize the tooth data. Students can help label the columns with the different numbers of teeth lost. Will they need a Zero column?

5. Students can place their teeth in the appropriate columns. They can also write a title such as *How Many Teeth Have We Lost?*

6. Hang the completed tooth graph in a place where the class can examine and share it.

Talking It Over

Discuss the graph. What does it show? What is the range of the numbers? Is there a number of teeth most students have lost? Why have some students lost a lot of teeth? (Look for possible age correlations.) What is the shape of the data? Will it stay the same all year? How will it look in June or another month?

More Teeth Fun

1. Students can survey other classes (younger or older) to determine how many teeth students in other classes have lost. They can display these graphs and compare the data from their own tooth findings.

2. With parental assistance, students can time how long it takes to brush their teeth. They can pool their data to make a class graph.

3. Students can sort and graph pictures of various animals (e.g., tiger, turtle, shark, bird, goldfish, butterfly) by whether or not they have teeth.

4. Read more tooth-related books, such as the following:

   • *Brushing Well* by Helen Frost and Gail Saunders-Smith (Pebble, 1999)

   • *Franklin and the Tooth Fairy* by Paulette Bourgeois (Scholastic, 1996)

   • *The Missing Tooth* by Joanna Cole (Random House, 1988)

   • *My Dentist, My Friend* by P. K. Hallinan (Ideal Children's, 1996)

   • *Tooth Fairy Magic* by Joanne Barkan (Cartwheel, 1995)

   The class can graph their favorite tooth-fairy books or illustrations. They can also make a class book about the tooth fairy and add imaginative pages showing what the fairy does with all the teeth it collects.

TV-Turnoff Week

"National TV-Turnoff Week" comes around every April. Challenge your children to turn off the tube for this activity and use their time (and minds) in different ways.

Materials

- ☑ Large pieces of chart paper or poster board
- ☑ Copies of Five-Column/Row Grid reproducible (page 140)
- ☑ Art paper
- ☑ Art supplies

Preparation

- Prepare a large six-column graph from the chart paper or poster board. Label the first five columns with numbers *0* to *4* and the sixth column *More*.

- Also prepare a five-column graph and label the columns for each day of the school week.

- Hand out copies of the *Five-Column/ Row Grid* reproducible. If you work with young children, print the days of the week and the number of hours in the columns before copying.

- With parental support, plan some great activities to do during "National TV-Turnoff Week."

Collecting and Graphing

1. Before "National TV-Turnoff Week," talk about TV viewing—how many hours the children watch TV, when they view, and their favorite programs and actors.

2. Brainstorm a class list of 25 activities children could do instead of watching television. Can they think of 50 ideas? 100? Students without televisions should have lots of ideas.

3. Provide students with grids and explain that they are going to graph the number of hours per week that they watch television. They can add data to their graphs each night before they go to bed. If you work with younger children, begin each day by asking if they watched television the day or night before and graph the information for them.

4. At the end of the week, students can pool their individual data to create a class graph showing how much TV they watch. If there are some children who don't have a television, they can put their names in the 0 column, unless they watch TV at a friend's house.

5. During "National TV-Turnoff Week," show the five-column graph and title it *Did You Watch TV This Week?* Each day, students can record whether or not they watched TV on the previous day (and night).

6. Display the completed television graphs for the class to share and examine.

Talking It Over

Discuss the graphs together. Before "National TV-Turnoff Week," did students watch more TV on certain days? Are they surprised by how much (or how little) TV they watch? How do they feel about "Turnoff Week"? What are their most popular activities to do instead of watching TV? Do they think their TV viewing habits will change? Why or why not?

More TV-Turnoff Fun

1. Enlist the support of other teachers and students and keep a whole-school graph to show how many students went without TV each day during this special week.

2. Students can graph how many hours they spend reading before TV-Turnoff Week and then collect the data again during TV-Turnoff Week. How do the graphs compare?

3. Have students interview older people who grew up without TV. What was it like? What did they do for fun? The children can make a class book titled *Instead of Watching TV, We Can...* and have everyone contribute a different idea and illustration.

4. Read stories about people who discover life without TV, such as the following:

   • *Aunt Chip and the Great Triple Creek Dam Affair* by Patricia Polacco (Philomel, 1996)

   • *Better Than TV* by Sara Swan Miller (Bantam, Doubleday, Dell, 1998)

   • *The Day the TV Blew Up* by Dan West (Albert Whitman, 1988)

   • *Fix-It* by David McPhail (Dutton, 1984)

   The class can graph their favorite stories about not watching TV, or about their favorite characters in one of these books.

5. Use other survey questions to find out (and graph) more about your students and television. Questions can include the following:

- How many hours a day is the TV on in your house? How many hours in a week?

- Is there more than one TV on at the same time in your house?

- How many televisions are in your home?

- Do you have a TV in your bedroom?

- Would you rather
  – watch TV or read a book?
  – watch TV or ride a bike?
  – watch TV or play with a friend?

- Did you watch TV before school today?

- What kind of TV shows do you like best? (Provide choices.)

- Do you think you watch too much TV?

- Would you like to participate in TV-Turnoff Week?

- Will you participate for one day? Two days? The whole week?

- Instead of watching TV, what would you most like to do? (For example, read a book, play with a friend, draw a picture, play a game, listen to music, ride a bike, use the computer, shoot hoops.)

6. Obtain information on "National TV-Turnoff Week" from

TV Turnoff Network
1611 Connecticut Avenue., NW
Suite 3A
Washington, D.C. 20009
(800) 939-6737
www.tvturnoff.org.

Up, Up, and Away!

Materials

- ☑ Large chart paper or poster board
- ☑ Student name cards or portraits
- ☑ Art paper
- ☑ Art supplies

Perform this simple and fun umbrella activity on a wet, rainy day. Ask students, *Did you bring an umbrella to school today?* and have them help you graph the responses.

Preparation

Prepare a large two-column graph from the chart paper or poster board. Add *Yes* and *No* labels, and title the graph *Did You Bring an Umbrella to School Today?*

Collecting and Graphing

1. Display the graph and place student name cards, portraits, or pieces of paper nearby.

2. As students arrive at school—or during "spare" moments on a long rainy day—have them place their names or portraits in the appropriate columns. Or, they can draw raindrops or umbrellas with their names and tape or glue them in the appropriate columns to complete the graph.

3. After students have responded, they can share and examine the completed graph.

Talking It Over

Talk about the graph together. What does the data show? How many children brought or didn't bring an umbrella today? How many more (or less) brought an umbrella than didn't bring one? Why? What does the data suggest about the weather? What would the graph look like during a different season? Why?

☔Our Umbrellas☔	
curved handle	X X X X X X X X
straight handle	X X X
plastic	X X X X
fabric	X X X X X X
solid color	X X X X
patterned	X X X X X X X X
opaque	X X X X X X X X X X
clear	X X
with cover	X X X X X

More Umbrella Fun

1. Students can sort and graph their umbrellas by attributes such as size, color, type of handle, patterns/plain, opaque/transparent, and plastic/fabric.

2. Help students survey how many umbrellas are in the whole school on a particular rainy day. They can also collect data on the types and colors of umbrellas or on who brought the most umbrellas—adults, younger children, girls, or boys. Encourage students to make some predictions before they conduct their surveys.

3. Take students for a walk outside in the rain, or just after the rain. Are there any dry areas? Why didn't these places get wet? What things outside serve as natural umbrellas?

4. Invite students to share and dramatize wet-weather poems such as the following:

   Rain on my house,
   Rain on my tree,
   Rain on my umbrella,
   But not on me!

   They can also use the poems to make little illustrated books.

5. Read and discuss books about umbrellas, such as the following:

   • *Maudie's Umbrella* by Kay Chorao (Dutton, 1975)

   • *My Red Umbrella* by Robert Bright (William Morrow, 1959)

   • *Umbrella* by Taro Yashima (Puffin, 1977)

   Students can graph their favorite umbrella stories, characters, or umbrella illustrations. They can also respond to specific questions about the literature.

6. If your school is located in an urban area, students can estimate how many umbrellas will pass the school in ten minutes. They can tally umbrellas and compare the total with their predictions. Talk about other kinds of data they may collect.

Valentine's Day

Do your students celebrate Valentine's Day? In this "hearty" activity, they can sort and graph colorful valentine cards. They can use the special cards they receive from their classmates, or, for even greater variety, valentines you've saved over the years.

Materials

☑ Large pieces of chart paper or poster board

☑ Valentine cards (e.g., used, homemade, store-bought)

☑ Two plastic hoops or jump ropes

☑ Heart stickers or stamps

☑ Art supplies

Preparation

● Prepare a large two-column graph from the chart paper or poster board.

● Ask students to bring valentines or to use those they receive for Valentine's Day at school.

Collecting and Graphing

1. Provide time for students to examine, share, and discuss the valentine cards.

2. Talk about Valentine's Day. What is it about? Who celebrates it? How? What do the children like best about Valentine's Day?

3. Display the two-column graph and valentine cards. Discuss the cards' attributes (e.g., lace/no lace, shape, color, glitter/no glitter, red/no red, cartoon characters/no cartoon characters, folded/flat). What do they have in common? What is different?

4. Offer a hypothesis about the cards for students to prove or disprove, such as *Most of the cards have red on them*.

5. Explain that students will need to work together to sort, classify, and organize their cards in order to prove or disprove your hypothesis. How can they do this?

6. Students can transfer their data (valentine cards) to the appropriate columns and glue or tape them in place. Or, they may use heart stickers, stamps, tally marks, or their own heart drawings to represent the cards.

7. Help students label the columns and add a title such as *Is Your Valentine Red?*

8. Display the completed valentine graph for the class to examine and share.

Talking It Over

Talk about the graph. What does the data show? Do most cards have red? Did students prove or disprove your hypothesis? Can they tell how many other colors were on the cards? How could they show that? What else did the graph show?

More Valentine Fun

1. Display a large two-column (or more) graph with a different valentine card or heart at the bottom of each column. At the top, write, *Which Valentine Do You Like Best?* Students can choose by placing heart stickers in the appropriate columns. Talk about their choices when they are finished.

2. Lay two plastic hoops or jump ropes in circles on the rug and display assorted valentines. Students can take turns grouping the cards and asking their classmates to guess their mystery sorting rules. They can even overlap the hoops to make three groups or a Venn diagram (page 136).

3. Distribute cups of assorted valentine candy. Have students graph the treats according to specific attributes (e.g., color, size, words/no words, chocolate/no chocolate). They can eat the data afterwards if other classmates have not handled the candy.

4. Display some heart-healthy snacks or invite students to bring some sugar-free treats from home. They can taste and graph their favorites and make a heart-shaped picture book about their healthy snacks.

Water Play—Sink or Float?

Materials

- ✔ Large pieces of chart paper or poster board
- ✔ Laminating film or self-adhesive plastic
- ✔ Large tray (optional)
- ✔ Masking tape (optional)
- ✔ Several objects that float and sink (e.g., balls, blocks, coins, pencils, shells, feathers, magnets, apples)
- ✔ Trays
- ✔ Large tub of water
- ✔ Art paper
- ✔ Art supplies

Water and children go well together—and so do science explorations and graphing. In this activity, students place objects in water to discover which sink or float, then graph the results.

Preparation

Prepare a large two-column graph from the chart paper or poster board. Label the columns *Sink* and *Float*. Laminate the graph or cover it with self-adhesive plastic. Or, use a large tray with a strip of masking tape as a column divider. Write *Sink* and *Float* in the two columns.

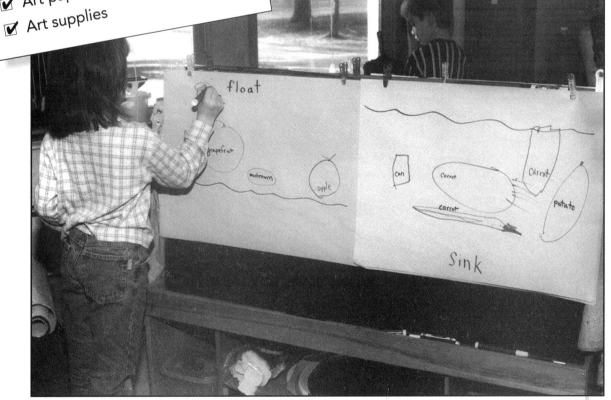

 © Fearon Teacher Aids FE111030

Collecting and Graphing

1. Gather the class around the tub of water. Have the assorted objects on a large tray and the *Sink or Float* graph nearby.

2. Invite students to predict if a particular object (e.g., a coin, a shell) will float or sink. Place the item in the tub of water and discuss what happens. Why did this occur?

3. Ask the class to examine the other objects near the tub. What will happen when these are placed in the water? Tell students that they will work with partners and test predictions about which items sink or float.

4. At their turn, students tell their partners what they think will happen and place one item at a time in the water. After testing each object, they can put it in the correct column on the *Sink or Float* graph or tray near the tub.

5. When finished, partners remove the items from the graph, return them to the tray, and let another pair take its turn.

6. After all the students have finished, they can make a more permanent record of their discoveries. Young children can draw individual or whole-class pictures of items that floated or sank. Older children can create a two-column graph and write the names of the items in the appropriate columns.

7. Display the completed graphs for the children to share and examine.

Talking It Over

Discuss what happened in the experiment and invite students to share their discoveries. Were there any surprises? Why did some objects sink? Why did some float? Why do some very heavy things float? Can students think of other objects that float or sink? Older children may talk about mass, density, and other factors that influence buoyancy.

More Water Fun

1. Provide students with a variety of materials with which to make boats (e.g., wood scraps, tuna cans, foil, sticks, modeling clay, paper, Styrofoam®, berry baskets). They can test and graph which boats sink or float. They can also estimate, graph, and discover how many pennies they can place in their boats before they sink!

2. Students can use different foods (e.g., a potato, a stick of celery, a grapefruit, a can of beans, a carrot) and test whether the items sink or float. They can graph their results—and may be surprised!

3. For homework, students can find and draw three things that float and three that sink. They can share their results with classmates and pool data to make a larger graph.

4. Help students graph results from other experiments. Students can test how objects absorb water or dissolve in water. They can also experiment to discover how quickly water evaporates.

5. Read books about water and flotation, such as the following:

   • *Amazing Boats* by Margaret Lincoln (Knopf, 1992)

   • *Ben Goes Swimming* by Jan Ormerod (HarperFestival, 2000)

   • *The Boat Alphabet Book* by Jerry Pallotta (Charlesbridge, 1998)

   • *Boat Book* by Gail Gibbons (Holiday House, 1983)

   • *Making Things Float and Sink* by Gary Gibson (Copper Beech, 1995)

   • *Sink or Float* by Lisa Trumbauer (Newbridge Communications, 1997)

   • *Who Sank the Boat?* by Pamela Allen (Putnam & Grosset, 1982)

   The class can graph their favorite water books and respond to specific water questions.

Do You Like Winter?

There are many wonderful ways to incorporate snowy-day activities into your math program. In this activity, students survey classmates and create a class graph to show how they would prefer to spend the winter if they were animals! You may coordinate this activity with a science unit on animals.

Materials

- ☑ Large chart paper or poster board
- ☑ Student portraits or name labels
- ☑ Art paper
- ☑ Art supplies

Preparation

● Prepare a large three-column graph from the chart paper or poster board. Label the columns *Sleep*, *Migrate*, and *Stay Active*. You may illustrate these labels by showing a sleeping boy, a girl fishing on a sunny beach, and a boy and girl sledding or building a snowman.

● Students can wear warm clothing and go for a winter walk to look for signs of animals.

Collecting and Graphing

1. Discuss how animals survive cold winter weather—by migrating to warmer areas, like whales and geese; by hibernating, like turtles and groundhogs; or by staying active, like foxes and rabbits. The children may even sing and move to this fun song:

(Tune: "Heads, Shoulders, Knees, and Toes")

Sleep, migrate, or stay active, stay active,
Sleep, migrate, or stay active, stay active,
Animals survive the winter this way
When they sleep, migrate, or stay active,
    stay active.

On *sleep*, the children close their eyes, press their hands together, and rest their cheeks on their hands. On *migrate*, they flap their hands as if flying south. On *stay active*, they jog in place. Start the song slowly and repeat it, getting faster each time!

2. Ask students how they would like to spend the winter if they were animals. Would they like to hibernate, migrate, or stay active? They may dramatize their choices and ask their friends to guess what they're doing.

3. Show students the prepared graph and talk about how to put their choices on the graph. They can attach their name labels or portraits in the columns of their choice or draw pictures of how they'd like to spend the winter and affix these in the appropriate columns.

4. Display the completed winter graph near the nature or science corner for students to examine and share. Place books and magazines about animals and winter nearby.

Talking It Over

Discuss the graph together. What does it show? Did students expect this? Which activity did most children choose? Why did they make their choices?

More Winter Fun

1. Help students survey their classmates about other winter activities such as building snow people, wearing winter clothing, sledding, and ice skating. They can use their data to make many wintry graphs!

2. Students can play a sorting game by grouping pictures of animals according to how they spend the winter. They may also collect and group pictures of winter clothing.

3. Enjoy books and magazines about animals in winter, such as the following:

   • *Animals in Winter* by Henrietta Bancroft and Richard G. Van Gelder (HarperCollins, 1997)

   • *Fox's Dream* by Tejima (Scholastic, 1987)

   • *When Winter Comes* by Robert Maass (Scholastic, 1993)

   Students can graph the funniest, strangest, or most curious winter critters. They can also answer specific nature questions.

4. Students can make bird feeders to care for their hungry winter friends. They can take their feeders home or hang them around the schoolyard. They can also graph the number of birds they attract and the treats the birds prefer!

Exercise!

Materials

☑ Copies of Ten-Column/Row Grid reproducible (page 142)

☑ Large pieces of chart paper or poster board

☑ Overhead projector (optional)

☑ Overhead projector transparency (optional)

☑ Overhead projector markers (optional)

☑ Recreational equipment as needed for each task

☑ Stopwatches or clocks

☑ Tape measures

☑ Folders (one per student)

☑ Art supplies

These exercise graphs get children actively involved in data collecting! In this lesson, students collect personal data about how they succeed with various physical tasks. Adapt the ideas as necessary for younger children and continue the activity all year by changing the exercises after a few weeks or months.

Preparation

● Hand out copies of the *Ten-Column/Row Grid* reproducible. Each student will need one grid for each exercise.

● Make a copy of the grid on an overhead transparency or prepare an enlarged copy on chart paper.

Collecting and Graphing

1. Ask students how many seconds they think they can balance on one foot. They can work in pairs to time each other. Use the overhead transparency grid or chart to show how to record times. How close were their estimates?

2. Explain that the class is going to have many opportunities to collect data from all sorts of fun physical tasks. Provide students with clipboards, folders, and grids to record their data.

3. Assign or help students choose several activities, such as the following:

   • For how many seconds can you balance on one leg?
   • How far can you throw a soft ball? A bean bag? A Frisbee®?
   • How far can you kick a soccer ball?
   • How many seconds does it take to run across the playground (or other field)?
   • How many jumping jacks (hops, sit-ups) can you do in one minute?
   • How many baskets can you shoot in one minute?
   • How far can you jump?
   • How long can you jump rope before missing?

4. Students can work in pairs as needed to set goals and help each other measure and record data. They can also work together to design their graphs to fit their activities. Students may need to do each activity beforehand in order to make their graphs fit their data. (For example, a student may make a daily count of the number of jumping jacks they can do in one minute or record the number of feet they can jump.)

5. Make sure all students feel emotionally safe to participate in these activities by encouraging them to support others, enforcing zero tolerance for teasing and ridicule, and allowing them to keep their data private or anonymous.

Talking It Over

As students perform their daily or weekly exercises, talk about the data. What about their goals? Do they expect to do better next time? How can they help make that happen? (Practice; ask advice.) After students complete their graphs, ask them to analyze their data. How did they do? Did their performances improve? Why or why not? What influenced their performances? (For example, a student may be ill, or it may be raining.)

More Exercise Fun

1. Have students keep journals to record and discuss their data and feelings about their exercises.

2. Play a fun and quick activity called "Mad Minute Math." The children can take turns performing chosen exercises for one minute. They can time themselves or their partners, and graph their data. Ideas may include

   • putting interlocking cubes together to make a "train"

   • counting beans or buttons from a large jar

   • hopping on one foot

   • jumping rope

   • writing their names

   • counting by rote

   • doing simple computation problems

   • writing numbers from 1 onward

   • writing a word for every letter of the alphabet (in order)

   • shooting baskets

   To avoid embarrassment, allow the children to keep their results and graphs private.

Have You Ever Had an X Ray?

In this activity, students complete a class graph to show who has and who has not had an X ray. You may use this idea when studying bones, hospitals, or other health-related subjects.

Materials

- ☑ Large chart paper or poster board
- ☑ Animal bones or skeletons
- ☑ X rays (obtained from hospitals, friends, parents)
- ☑ Student name cards or portraits
- ☑ Art supplies

Preparation

Prepare a large two-column graph from the chart paper or poster board. Label the columns *Yes* and *No* and write the title *Have You Ever Had an X Ray?*

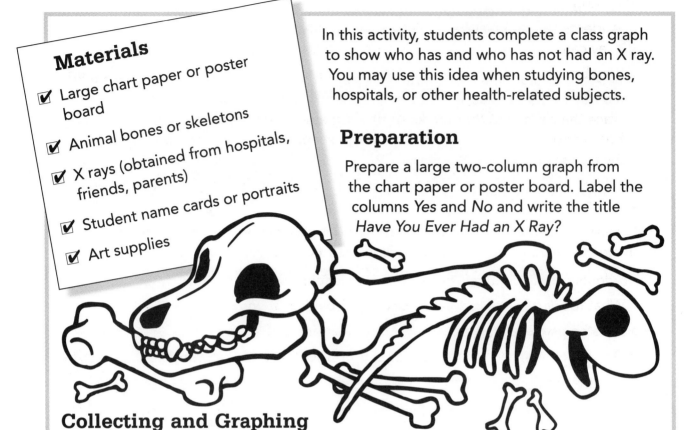

Collecting and Graphing

1. Display a "mystery" animal bone or skeleton and ask students to guess what it is. Talk about bones. Why do people need them? Can they be broken?

2. Hold up a real X ray and place it against a window or other light source to enhance visibility. Ask students if they know what it is. When do people get X rays? (When they break a bone, swallow something accidentally, or have their teeth checked.) Which students have had X rays? How could the class make a graph to show who has and who has not had an X ray?

3. Show students the graph and invite them to take turns putting their names in the *Yes* or *No* columns. Since some children may not know whether they have had an X ray, they will need to ask their parents when they get home. Let the students know that it will be OK to change the data the next day.

4. Display the completed X ray graph for the class to examine and share.

Talking It Over

Discuss the graph together. What does the data show? How many children have or have not had an X ray? Invite students to tell why they had an X ray. What if they surveyed a younger grade? An older class? Would they get the same results? Why or why not?

More Bony Fun

1. Organize some simple activity centers for students to explore bones, such as the following:

   • Students can make paper skeletons, using brads to make movable joints. They can count and graph the number of bones in their skeletons.

   • Bury bones in the sand table (or in a tub of sand) for "paleontologists" to dig up. Students can count the number of bones they find and time each other's efforts!

   • Trace the shapes of real animal bones (e.g., deer, cow, chicken) on poster board and have students match bones to shapes. They can also try matching the bones to pictures of animals.

   Students can make graphs of their favorite "bony" activities to display near the centers.

2. Display foods for healthy bones (e.g., sardines, cheese, yogurt, broccoli) and invite the children to choose and graph their favorites.

3. Students can respond to "bony" survey questions such as the following:

   • What foods help make healthy bones? (Provide options.)

   • Who helps us keep our bones healthy? (Provide options.)

   • Do you know what a (name of bone) is or does? (Provide options.)

   • Do you know what a (name of body organ) is or does? (Provide options.)

   • Have you ever stayed in a hospital?

   • Have you ever been to the emergency room?

   • What vaccinations have you had? (Provide options.)

   • What people work in hospitals? (Provide options.)

   • Would you like to work in a hospital?

4. Read bone-related books, such as the following:

   • *The Big Book of Bones: An Introduction to Skeletons* by Claire Llewellyn (Scholastic, 1998)

   • *Bones, Our Skeletal System* by Seymour Simon (Morrow Jr. Books, 1998)

   • *Curious George Goes to the Hospital* by Margaret and H. A. Rey (Scholastic, 1966)

   • *Funnybones* by Janet and Allan Ahlberg (Mulberry, 1980)

   The class can graph their most popular "bony" books or illustrations.

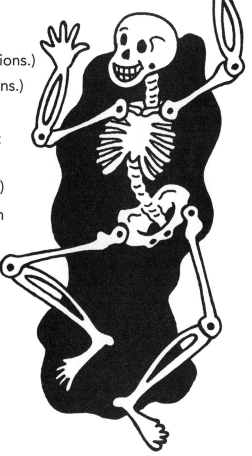

"Yes or No" Graphs

"Yes or No" graphs are useful because they're quick and simple. They have only two columns, making data easy to collect and interpret, and can be used with mathematicians of all ages. Use "Yes or No" graphs to connect questions to topics being explored in any curriculum area. (For example, *Have you ever been to the ocean? Have you heard of Susan B. Anthony? Should the Rainbow Fish have given away its scales?*) But remember that "Yes or No" graphs can sometimes limit the depth of children's mathematical thinking. Be sure to offer other graphing experiences.

Materials

- ☑ Large pieces of chart paper or poster board
- ☑ Laminating film or self-adhesive plastic
- ☑ Student name cards or portraits
- ☑ Wooden clothespins
- ☑ Art supplies

Preparation

● Prepare several large two-column graphs from the chart paper or poster board. Label the columns *Yes* and *No*. Laminate or cover the graphs with self-adhesive plastic. Write a target question at the top of each day's graph.

● Use this list of possible "Yes or No" ideas as springboards for your own questions. Also invite students to help think of class survey questions.

- Did you have hot cereal (waffles, toast, cold cereal) for breakfast?

- Did you bring a lunch box today?

- Did you bring a snowsuit today?

- Did you notice your paintings in the hall?

- Do you know when Dr. Martin Luther King, Jr., was born?

- Have you ever read *The Wind in the Willows*?

- Do you know what a fraction is?

- Do you know the name of this shape? (For example, show a pyramid.)

- Can you think of seven (or more) different ways to make 25 cents? (Provide coins, paper, and pencils at a nearby table.)

– Would you like a turn with the computer today?

– Are you coming to Open House tonight?

– Do you know why we celebrate Memorial Day?

– Will our seeds sprout today?

– Do you know in what year you were born?

– Have you ever ice skated?

– Do you know what you call a cat that drinks lemonade? (Riddles are fun!)

● Keep the data anonymous in situations where children may feel embarrassed by responses (e.g., Did you remember your homework?).

Collecting and Graphing

1. Display a "Yes or No" graph and its target question. Provide means for recording the data nearby (e.g., student name cards, portraits, clothespins).

2. Older children can complete the graphs themselves, while younger children can help each other read the questions.

Talking It Over

Always discuss each "Yes or No" graph. What does the data show? Did more children answer yes or no? Why? Invite students to explain their choices or decisions. How can they use this information? What other questions may they ask?

More "Yes or No" Fun

1. At the top of one "Yes or No" graph, write *What Did You Do This Weekend?* Use this graph on Monday mornings to ask questions about the weekend, such as "Did you ride your bike?"

2. Hand out copies of the *Survey* reproducible (page 133). Students can survey their classmates with their own "Yes or No" questions, create graphs, and write or talk about their findings.

What Did You Do This Weekend?	Penny H. YES	Penny H. NO	Brad O. YES	Brad O. NO	Charles T. YES	Charles T. NO	Lisa M. YES	Lisa M. NO	A__ YES	A__ NO	Kim B. YES	Kim B. NO
Travel		✔	✔		✔							✔
Rollerskate		✔		✔	✔							✔
Ride Bike		✔	✔		✔						✔	
Movie		✔	✔				✔					
Friends	✔				✔	✔						
Read	✔				✔		✔		✔		✔	
Computer	✔			✔			✔		✔		✔	

All Zipped Up!

Materials

- ✔ Mrs. Toggle's Zipper by Robin Pulver (Four Winds, 1990)
- ✔ Large chart paper or poster board
- ✔ Art paper or plain index cards
- ✔ Sticky notes
- ✔ Art supplies

Zippers are lots of fun—and most children wear them. In this activity, students count all of the zippers in their possession and add those numbers to a class zipper graph. Plan this lesson for a cold day so they can include winter coats, snowsuits, and backpacks in the count.

Preparation

Read and enjoy *Mrs. Toggle's Zipper*—the story of a woman whose zipper jams and traps her inside her coat!

Collecting and Graphing

1. Talk about zippers. Why do people use them? Where can you find zippers? Write a list; include items like *purses, boots, sleeping bags, suitcases, pillow casings*, and *wallets*.

2. Without looking, have each student estimate how many zippers he or she is wearing. Also ask students to estimate how many zippers they brought to school. Can they think where they might find their zippers? Have them write estimates on paper before they actually count.

3. Model how to count all of the zippers you brought to school today. You may include your clothes, coat, handbag, briefcase, and wallet. Keep track of zippers as you count by making check or tally marks on the board.

4. Provide each pair of children with paper. Pairs can take turns counting zippers and making check or tally marks on paper, then transfering the totals to sticky notes or index cards.

5. Display the chart paper or poster board and let students suggest how to organize the data to make a graph. Try some of their ideas.

6. Guide students through the process of arranging sticky notes or index cards in vertical columns on the paper. They can start with zero and move from left to right, working up to the highest number. If there are really high numbers, discuss the possibility of adding a *More Than* column.

7. Students can help add column lines, labels, and a title such as *How Many Zippers Do We Have Today?*

8. Display the completed zipper graph for the class to examine and share.

Talking It Over

Talk about the graph. What does the data show? How close were students' estimates? Were there any surprises? Is there a wide range of numbers, or does the same number occur frequently? Why do some children have so many zippers? Who brought the most zippers to school today? Ask that child to bring out his or her coat and backpack to show all of the zippers. What would happen if this data was collected in a different season? Would the numbers be different? How? Why?

More Zipper Fun

1. Display a large two-column graph titled *Are You Wearing a Zipper Today?* Students can record a *yes* or *no* response when they first enter the classroom. Discuss the results together.

2. For homework, students can survey their families and find out how many zippers each family member is wearing. How many are worn altogether in each family? The children can create their own graphs or use copies of reproducible grids to record data about their family members (pages 139–141). Compare and discuss the data in class. Why were some families wearing more zippers than others? Do those families have more members?

3. Begin a class list that shows all of the places where students might find zippers. Encourage them to continue adding to the list as an independent activity. For greater challenge, older children can try to find all of the zippers in their closets, or in their entire houses. They can make a class graph of the total number of zippers or record the places where zippers were found (e.g., on furniture or clothing).

© Fearon Teacher Aids FE111030

Apples

Birthday Cake

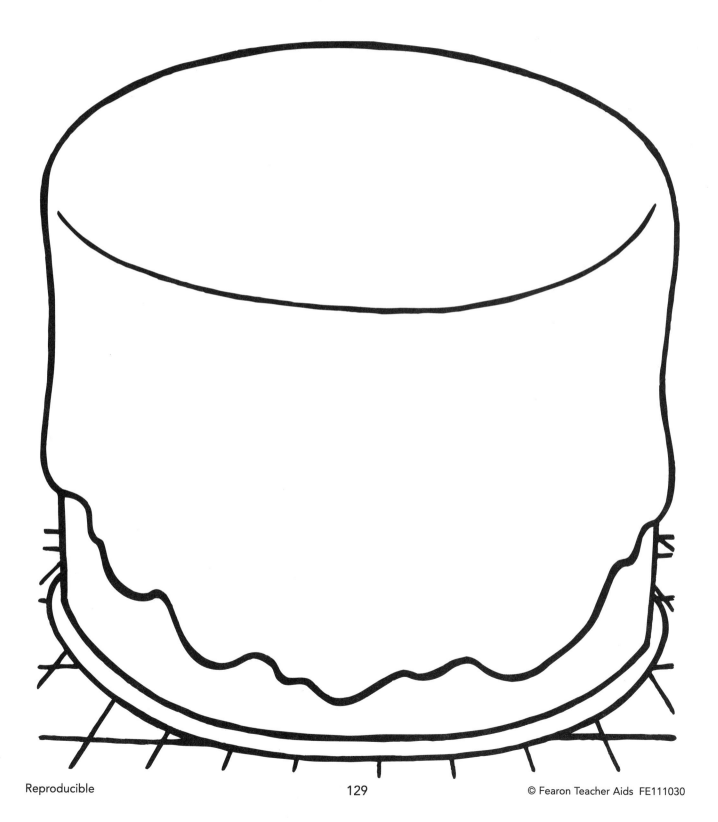

Eyes

_____   _____

_____   _____

_____   _____

Hands

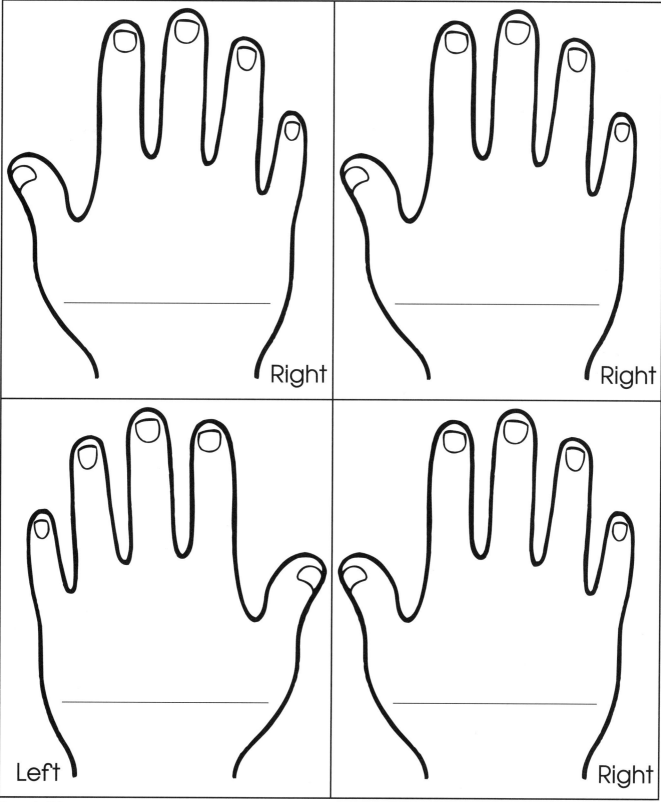

Right

Right

Left

Right

Ice Cream Scoops

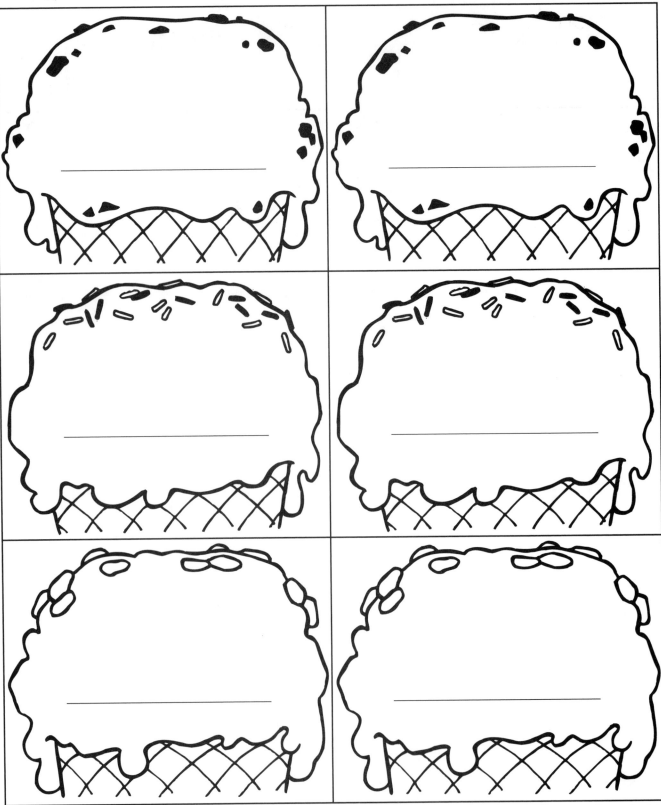

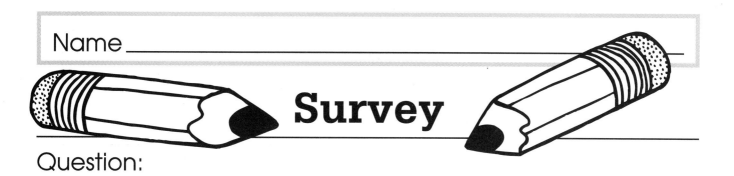

Name _____

Survey

Question:

Take Me to School

Feet

Bicycle

Car

Van

Bus

Other

Teeth

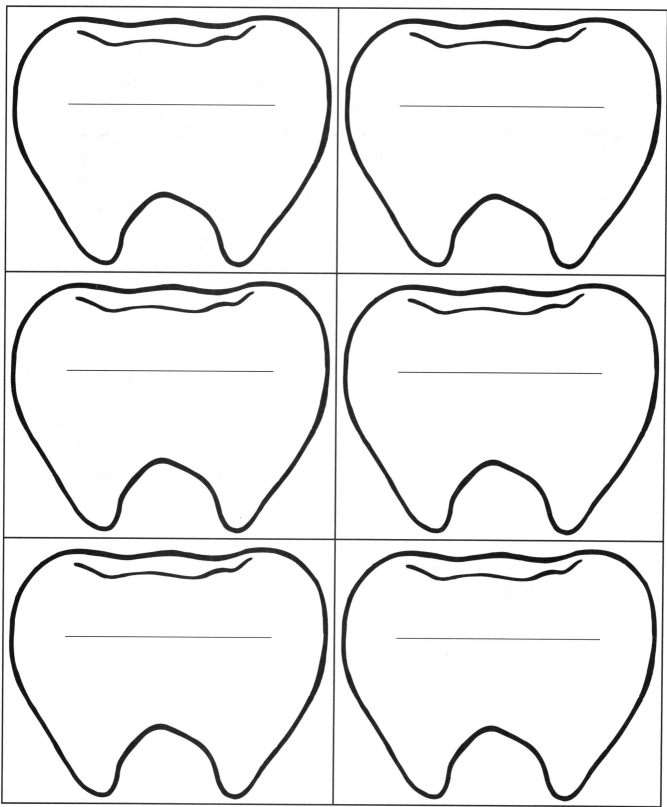

Venn Diagram

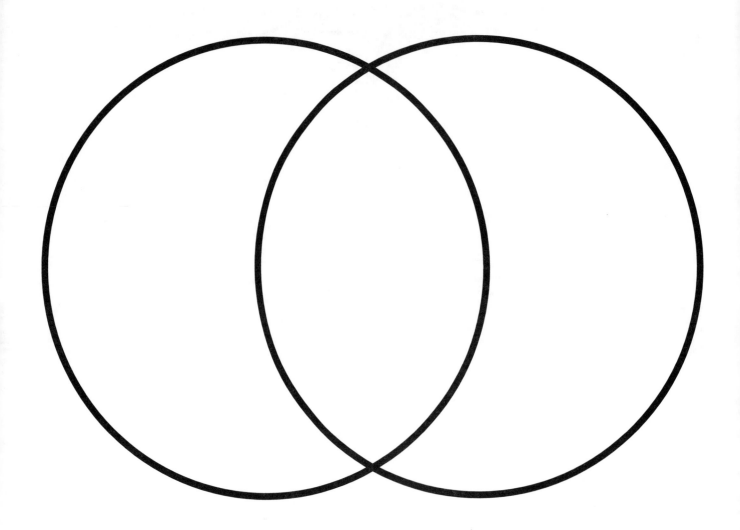

Two-Column/Row Grid

(Use this grid horizontally or vertically.)

137

Three-Column/Row Grid

(Use this grid horizontally or vertically.)

Four-Column/Row Grid

(Use this grid horizontally or vertically.)

Five-Column/Row Grid

(Use this grid horizontally or vertically.)

Six-Column/Row Grid

(Use this grid horizontally or vertically.)

Ten-Column/Row Grid

(Use this grid horizontally or vertically.)

Parent Letter

Dear Families,

This year, your children will be immersed in the wonderful world of graphing! They will participate in lots of fun activities and learn many important math skills, such as counting, sorting, problem solving, and communicating ideas.

We want you to know about the graphing activities so that you can talk to your children about them. You may be asked to help your children collect data. They will appreciate your interest! They may have to measure the feet of family members or count how many seconds it takes to brush their teeth. They may survey the ages of people in your house, the number of pets, or even the number of windows.

As your children collect data, they will need to record it in some way. You may see them writing tally marks on pieces of paper or completing survey sheets. In any case, please encourage your children to do as much for themselves as possible as they gather the data, write it down, and organize it into a graph.

Since your children will need to be able to sort and classify data, you can help them strengthen their skills by sorting things together. Perhaps you could take turns sorting buttons or little toys and guessing each other's sorting rules. Ask your children to explain their reasons for sorting and classifying and encourage them to talk about their surveys after they've shared their data at school. Your support will be really motivating!

May you and your children enjoy the fun and fascinating world of graphing!

Sincerely,

Graphing Resources

1. The National Council of Teachers
   of Mathematics, Inc. (NCTM)
   1906 Association Drive
   Reston, VA 20191-9988
   (703) 620-9840
   www.nctm.org

2. Dale Seymour Publications
   4350 Equity Drive
   P.O. Box 2649
   Columbus, OH 43216
   (800) 321-3106
   www.pearsonlearning.com

3. ETA/Cuisenaire
   500 Greenview Court
   Vernon Hills, IL 60061
   (800) 445-5985
   www.etacuisenaire.com

4. U.S. Toy Company/
   Constructive Playthings
   13201 Arrington Road
   Grandview, MO 64030
   (800) 841-6478
   www.ustoy.com

5. Oriental Trading Company
   P.O. Box 3407
   Omaha, NE 68103-0407
   (800) 246-8400
   www.oriental.com

6. Tom Snyder Productions
   80 Coolidge Hill Rd
   Watertown, MA 02472
   (800) 342-0236
   www.teachtsp.com